£2.75

Practical social sciences

International Library of Sociology

Founded by Karl Mannheim

Editor: John Rex, University of Warwick

Arbor Scientiae
Arbor Vitae

A catalogue of the books available in the **International Library of Sociology** and other series of Social Science books published by Routledge & Kegan Paul will be found at the end of this volume.

Practical social sciences

Adam Podgórecki
Professor of Sociology, University of Warsaw

Routledge & Kegan Paul
London and Boston

*First published in 1975
by Routledge & Kegan Paul Ltd
Broadway House, 68–74 Carter Lane,
London EC4V 5EL and
9 Park Street
Boston, Mass. 02108, USA
Set in Monotype Times
and printed in Great Britain by
Butler & Tanner Ltd, Frome and London*

© *Adam Podgórecki 1975*

*No part of this book may be reproduced in
any form without permission from the
publisher, except for the quotation of brief
passages in criticism*

ISBN 0 7100 8175 8

Contents

	Preface	vii
	Introduction	1
part one	**The theoretical and practical sciences**	7
1	The notion of valuation	9
2	What is the concern of the practical sciences?	20
3	The practical natural sciences and the practical social sciences	23
part two	**A description of the practical social sciences**	25
4	The course of purposive procedure	27
5	Elements of projective procedure	46
6	The corrective and preventive procedures	67
7	The analytic–normative reasoning process	76
part three	**Conclusions**	89
8	Values and realization: the equation of the ideal and the real	91

9	Methodology of the practical social sciences and social engineering	100
	Notes	122
	Index	132

Preface

This book, *Practical Social Sciences*, is based on my previous works. I have tried here to present only research and studies which were earlier published in Polish in the following books: *Characteristics of Practical Sciences* (1962), *Principles of Social Engineering* (1966), and series of books which I edited: *Sociotechnics (Practical Uses of Sociology)* (1968), *Sociotechnics (Efficiency of Actions)* (1970), *Sociotechnics (Styles of Interaction)* (1972).

I am indebted to my colleagues of the Section on Social Engineering of the Polish Sociological Association who, before, and since, the establishment of this Section in 1964 were kind enough to discuss with me various aspects of problems and issues connected with macro- and micro-decision making, utilization of social sciences and methodology of practical social sciences.

I am also grateful to the Center for Advanced Study in the Behavioral Sciences at Stanford for giving me (during the academic year 1972–3 as a Fellow of this Center) the opportunity to prepare this book for publication. Many warm thanks are due to Miriam Gallaher who used her extraordinary skills to do the editorial work and to Mary Tye who was kind enough to type the book and be nice to me at the same time. The essential part of this book was translated from Polish into English by Dr P. Graff.

ADAM PODGÓRECKI

To Robert Merton

Introduction

There are many different classifications of sciences.[1] Ampère divided them into sciences of the material world and sciences of the psychic world. The sciences of the material world are divided, according to him, into sciences of inorganic matter (those, in turn, are classified into mathematical and physical sciences) and into sciences of organic matter (classified into natural science and medicine). The sciences of the psychic world are divided into sciences of individual psychic matters and the social sciences. As we know, Comte classified the sciences into the basic ones, inquiring into laws (mathematics, mechanics, physics, chemistry, biology, sociology), and the derivative ones, inquiring into objective phenomena. Spencer distinguished abstract, abstract-concrete, and concrete sciences; Wundt distinguished detailed (formal and real) and philosophical disciplines. The real sciences Wundt divided into natural and human; the natural sciences were classified into phenomenological, systematic and genetic ones, as were the human disciplines. Windelband, generally speaking, distinguished the natural and the human disciplines, and Rickert's classification was into those disciplines dealing with nature and those with culture.

The remarkable feature of all these classifications is that they are all principally divisions of the theoretical disciplines, i.e. of those which describe that which is there. They fail to include the practical sciences, i.e. those which are concerned with prescriptions for action. Thus the latter are left outside the scope of the attempts at general classifications of sciences.

The idea that the practical sciences (prescriptive sciences) ought to be recognized as a separate group was expressed for the first time by Aristotle. It was developed by Francis Bacon in his division of the philosophy of nature into the speculative and the operative: the former inquired into laws, the latter applied them. In more recent

1

times this concept was elaborated again by K. Menger[2] and L. Petrażycki.[3]

According to Petrażycki, the fundamental division is between the theoretical and practical sciences. The former deal with what is, the latter with what ought to be done. The theoretical disciplines are divided into general sciences, covering all the objects which bear the given characteristics studied by the given science, and individual sciences, i.e. those which deal with only some of the objects bearing the given characteristics. The individual disciplines are further subdivided into descriptive sciences, describing their objects as they are at the moment when a description is made, and historical disciplines, presenting their objects in their chronological development. On the other hand, the practical sciences are subdivided into normative (essential, basic), i.e. those which recommend or reject some types of action as such, and teleological, which recommend or reject some types of action as proper or improper means to the assumed ends.

Such a classification of sciences facilitates their orderly arrangement: it helps to reveal the links and differences between scientific disciplines and points to the similarities and differences in the methods used in them. Within this framework, general sciences are, for example, physics, psychology, sociology, economics, etc. Descriptive disciplines are geography, zoology, demography, etc. Among the historical sciences are history of geography, history of medicine, history of law, etc. As examples of normative sciences we have ethics and grammar. Finally, the teleological disciplines are such fields of inquiry as medicine, technology, legal policy, social engineering.[4]

The common feature of all of the above classifications is that they distinguish the practical sciences as a separate group. W. Biegański,[5] and in particular K. Krzeczkowski,[6] present a number of arguments to justify the validity and the practical need for such a distinction. Many important arguments along the same lines can also be found in works by G. Hostelet.[7]

The most significant arguments can be summarized as follows. The practical disciplines make use of methods different from those of the theoretical ones, and thus it is necessary to analyze their peculiarities and their validity. Science in general (and the social sciences in particular) is more and more concerned not only with elucidation of reality, but with analysis of how to change it, so that there arises the need for a methodological analysis of the limits of change. The practical sciences take account of value judgments, which are a significant part of social life, while the theoretical sciences neither approve nor disapprove of phenomena. Finally, the practical sciences have their own peculiar problems which they have to apprehend and elucidate.

Apart from those arguments which do not seem to require more detailed justifications, a special consideration should be emphasized. The logic of conscious ways of the shaping of law as one of the essential means of social reconstruction is important enough to make an analysis of the peculiarities of the practical disciplines worthwhile; in particular, it is important enough that we should attempt to gain an insight into the efficiency of their methods.

R. K. Merton has noted:[8]

> In some one of its numerous forms, the problem of the unanticipated consequences of purposive action has been treated by virtually every substantial contributor to the long history of social thought. The diversity of context and variety of terms by which this problem has been known, however, have tended to obscure the definite continuity in its consideration. In fact, this diversity of context—ranging from theology to technology—has been so pronounced that not only has the substantial identity of the problem been overlooked, but no systematic, scientific analysis of it has as yet been effected.

This problem will have to be analyzed for the sake of the validity of the newly emerging discipline—the policy of law. For we have to concede that 'legislators are also only human beings, and they are laymen in technical matters.'*[9]

Another reason for undertaking an inquiry into the methods of the practical sciences is the fact that there are very few works dealing with the matter. In American science, which has done the most towards investigating methodology, elaborations devoted directly to the methodology of the practical disciplines do not appear.[10] Many researches have been carried out which may be helpful for explicating the methodology of the practical sciences, but the methodology itself has been almost wholly neglected. Such investigations, carried out on different levels of abstraction, are pursued by American researchers without any attention to their methodological uniformity. These possibly relevant fields of investigation include the methods of social research, the theory of games and decision making, the science of administration, the science of management, the role of value judgments in social sciences, and discussions of application of the methods of social research to various fields of social life.

The methods of social research are well covered in American literature. Among the most valuable works are M. Jahoda, M. Deutsch and S. W. Cook, *Research Methods in Social Relations* (a basic work, containing perhaps the best bibliography of the subject);[11] L. Festinger and D. Katz, *Research Methods in the Behavioral*

---

* Where I lack access to the original source an asterisk (*) is inserted before the reference number. Where there is no asterisk the quotation is reproduced verbatim.

Sciences,[12] T. C. McCormick and R. G. Francis, *Methods of Research in the Behavioral Sciences*.[13]

Recently, the theory of games and decision making has been rapidly developing. Its problems concern individual and group decision making; certainty, uncertainty and risk as factors modifying the process of decision making; etc. The general assumption underlying these inquiries is that the more empirical research is, the less need there is for abstract theory. The basic books in this field are R. D. Luce and H. Raiffa, *Games and Decisions* (with a systematic bibliography);[14] J. L. Savage, *The Foundations of Statistics*;[15] H. W. Kuhn and W. W. Tucker, 'Theory of games,'[16] and 'Linear inequalities and related systems' (on linear programing);[17] D. Blackwell and M. A. Girshick, *Theory of Games and Statistical Decisions*;[18] W. Edwards, 'The theory of decision making' (a statistical theory of decisions and a theory of utility).[19] In Polish literature, some of the related problems are discussed in Oskar Lange, *Ekonomia polityczna*,[20] chapters 4 and 5.

There are many American studies devoted to the improvement of private and public management and administration, some taking the standpoint of maximum social effectiveness in that they try to find the means of securing social acceptance for newly introduced patterns of human interrelations. The basic works of this type are H. A. Simon, *Models of Man*;[21] R. Ackoff, *The Design of Social Research*;[22] C. W. Churman, R. Ackoff and E. L. Ackoff, *Introduction to Operations Research*;[23] H. A. Simon, D. W. Smithburg and V. A. Thompson, *Public Administration*;[24] A. H. Leighton, *The Governing of Man*.[25]

A separate and very large field in which some methodological elaborations (e.g. methods of interviewing the employees) and several problem researches (such as analyses of relations between institutions) can be found is that of work organization. Among the numerous works two relatively recent books are outstanding: H. J. Chruden, *Personnel Management*[26] and J. H. Taylor, *Personnel Administration*.[27]

The problem of values has been investigated from many points of view, though that which would be the most significant for the methodology of the practical sciences is by no means predominant. The following works by T. Parsons should be mentioned: *The Social System*,[28] *Structure of Social Action*,[29] 'The place of ultimate values in sociological theory';[30] the most interesting work by Parsons (in collaboration with E. A. Shils) is *Toward a General Theory of Action*,[31] especially Part II, Values, Motives, and Systems of Action. Among works by other authors are H. Becker, *Through Values to Social Interpretation*;[32] H. Becker, *Man in Reciprocity*;[33] Mukerjee Radhakamal, *Social Structure of Values*;[34] W. L. Kolf, 'The Changing Prominence of Values in Modern Sociological Theory';[35] A. M.

Rose, *Theory and Method in the Social Sciences*;[36] P. H. Furley, 'Sociological Science and the Problem of Values';[37] E. Benoit-Smullyan, 'Value judgments and social science.'[38] These works deal with the role of values in social life, with the factors which determine the choice of subjects for study, with problems of the responsibility of scientists, with semantic and ontological analyses of such concepts as value, deed, action, etc.

Another field in which much material can be found for the methodology of the practical sciences is that of applied social science. Three books that can be mentioned in this connection are: H. Zeisel, H. Kalven, Jr, and B. Buchholz, *Delay in the Court*,[39] devoted to analysis of the methods of improving the work of courts of law; W. A. R. Leys, *Ethics for Policy Decisions*,[40] dealing with assumptions in and determinants of political and legal decisions; F. K. Beutel, *Some Potentialities of Experimental Jurisprudence as a New Branch of Social Science*,[41] discussing the problem of experiment in the legal sciences. Scattered among many other works are interesting considerations that can be useful for the methodology of the practical sciences. Their general direction is traced in a paper by R. K. Merton, 'The role of applied social sciences in the formation of policy.'[42] Merton grouped research problems according to their practical application in terms of the following classification by the Applied Social Science Bureau of Columbia University:

1. *Diagnostic*: Determining whether action is required. . . .
2. *Prognostic*: Forecasting trends to plan for future needs. . . .
3. *Differential Prognosis*: Determining choice between alternative policies. . . .
4. *Evaluative*: Appraising effectiveness of action program. . . .
5. *General Background Data*: Of general utility or serving diverse purposes. . . .
6. *'Educative' Research*: Informing publics upon pertinent data and particularly countering misconceptions.

'Strategic Fact-Finding:' this involves the systematic assembling of descriptive data pertinent for popular conceptions and controversial beliefs.

To conclude these introductory remarks on the divisions of science, I would like to point out that if we compare the theoretical and the practical sciences, we can easily see that the theoretical sciences, and the formal disciplines in particular, have clear logical structures, whereas the practical sciences are marked by a multitude of unknown factors and of undetermined relations between their parts. It is thus necessary to bring some order into the concepts and rules employed by the practical sciences, and the fact that so much is unclear in them obliges us to particular methodological care. For, according to an ancient Rhetorician (St Augustine), 'A thing need not be true because it is badly worded; nor is it false because it is splendidly phrased.'

The postulate of tying theory to practice is sufficient motive for undertaking methodological inquiry into the practical disciplines. The theoretical sciences seek to determine the relationships between things; practical activity consists in applying what they have taught us. Thus, it is of particular importance for social life that we have a theory of practice so as to transport scientific knowledge from the descriptive sciences to the side of action in such manner that errors will be avoided and the intended objectives will be attained. To connect theory and practice means, among other things, to conceptualize and formalize the necessary regularities and corollaries between them.

The notions of value and of valuations play quite an important role in the methodology of the practical social sciences. They constitute the necessary and strategical elements of sciences of this type. Nevertheless a lot of misunderstandings and misinterpretations have accumulated as far as the meanings of these basic concepts are concerned. The metaphysical and the methodological points of view are constantly and systematically confused whenever the social sciences are discussed. Untestable meanings of a metaphysical kind incessantly interfere with the methodological point of view. Let us leave aside the metaphysical aspects of those meanings and concentrate on those which have methodological significance.

In trying to solve the questions of methodology of the practical social sciences it is necessary to analyze at least three fundamental problems: (a) the meaning of the notion of valuation, (b) the methodology of all possible practical activities, and (c) the strategies of change at the level of social sciences development. The present book will pursue an analysis of these problems by means of a triptych-like structured approach.

One might raise several objections against terms, 'theoretical sciences' and 'practical sciences,' and one might propose, for example, different notions like 'descriptive sciences' and 'prescriptive sciences.' Still the term 'descriptive sciences' seems to be too narrow: it omits explanatory functions of social sciences and comes to close in the scientific deviation which is called 'flat empiricism.' 'Prescriptive sciences,' on the other hand, might suggest unilateral obedience to the recommendations and this is not always the case. Neither does the term 'applied sciences' solve the problems. The concept of applied science emphasizes the application of findings which have been discovered by the basic sciences but omits, at the same time, the problem of the procedure of this application. It seems to be quite clear that the crucial problem of sciences which are opposite to the theoretical sciences is what could well be called the 'theory of practice.'

part one

The theoretical and practical sciences

1 The notion of valuation

Descriptive proposition and valuational proposition

The epistemological problem, formulated as 'What is valuation?,' is admittedly one of the most difficult gnoseological questions. So far any attempts to specify the meaning of this notion seem to have resulted merely in increasing the number of relevant interpretations. Yet, the problem of the cognitive character of valuation is, certainly, interesting not only from a purely theoretical point of view, but also because of a number of significant implications for various domains involved in any given interpretation of valuation. Law is one of the most important such domains. Valuations are inherent in law. The cognitive specificity of law is constituted by the methodological specificity of valuations. Nevertheless—in spite of these generally accepted opinions—I assume as a fundamental thesis the opinion that it is an illusion to think that the methodological character of valuational propositions differs from that of descriptive propositions.

Maria Ossowska points to two basic criteria of distinguishing valuational propositions from descriptive ones. These are: the use of relevant predicative words, and the approving or disapproving character of the utterance.[1] Thus we can distinguish valuational propositions from descriptive propositions by the presence or absence therein of the predicative word 'good,' or 'bad.' To say that Mr X is a good citizen, or a bad Catholic, means that Mr X's behavior or his opinions are such that a certain valuation of his civic or religious attitude can be made. The predicative words 'good' and 'bad' generally do not appear in descriptive propositions.

In certain cases when valuational propositions use the predicative words 'good' and 'bad,' these state that the qualities designated by them are appropriate as a means to an end. Such is, for example, the statement that in certain instances a candle may provide good ski wax. For a gourmet a fat chicken is a good chicken, but fat ham is bad ham; or, a good watchdog should be vicious. These are examples quoted by Ziembiński.[2] On the other hand, a number of propositions in which the predicative word 'good' or 'bad' does not occur are, nevertheless, intuitively treated as valuations, such statements, in a variety of forms, imply approval or disapproval.[3] This can be done *expressis verbis*, for example by declaring 'Mr Y is an egoist'; by the tone of the utterance; by the attendant gesture; or by the structure of the utterance which—seemingly praising—may, in fact, through the arrangement of its elements express disapproval.

Whatever the form of a valuational proposition, there is a marked difference between a descriptive and a valuational utterance. Thus not only in the methodology of sciences but in daily life, the mechanism of shifting from the plane of description to that of valuation, and the direct transfer from the language of valuation to that of description, is sensed as passing to another, distinct semantic category. If a jurist *should* be a good legal adviser or judge, it does not follow that he *is* one. Similarly, from the fact that a man is a rascal successfully pretending to be an honest man, it does not follow that this should be so. As in colloquial usage, so in the language of the social sciences, passing from the category of description to that of valuation without acknowledging valuational assumptions is considered unjustified. In the methodology of social sciences valuations tend to be eliminated wherever possible, and when this seems impracticable or hard to attain it is explicitly stated that given utterances are not descriptive but valuational. The gulf between what is and what should be cannot be crossed.

The distinction between these two notions is particularly clear in law and morality. For instance, from the proposition 'Acts or default on the part of a debtor in a joint and several obligation can not be detrimental to the interests of co-debtors' (Article 371 of the Polish Civil Code) it does not follow that what such a debtor does will not be to the detriment of his co-debtors. He may happen to take such steps as will make his co-debtors sustain a loss. The provision in question does not establish what can not happen in actual fact, but a normative 'may not.' It provides that in case one of the co-debtors in a joint and several obligation brings about such a loss, he should compensate the affected co-debtors. From the proposition that the husband can not commit rape upon his wife (Article 204.1 of the Polish Penal Code) it does not follow that husbands do not do so now and then. The normative and the factual meaning of a term—like 'can' in the case above—frequently happen to be entirely different.

In this situation the question arises again: 'What is the cognitive nature of valuational propositions?' If we disregard various *sensu stricto* epistemological problems involved, the cognitive nature of descriptive propositions is a fairly simple problem. Such propositions —when they are not tautological—are more or less general descriptions of reality. Thus the reality—either external or internal—is itself the reference point for the statement which purports to describe the reality. Is the position of valuational propositions in any way similar? Does it make sense to say that valuational propositions somehow reflect the reality to which they refer?

Undoubtedly, such statements as 'Mr A is an outcast of society' or 'Miss B is beautiful' do not reflect reality. This is so because Mr A may seem queer to some people, but others may treat him as a normal person; Miss B may be fascinating to one man, but repulsive to another. So as to make this an autotelic semantic discussion, we could say that descriptive propositions purport to present reality as it is (irrespective of the subject perceiving it), whereas valuational propositions express a relationship of the subject to the reality. Yet such a statement would but seemingly be in keeping with the relevant intuitions. Is the observation of an object and its description not a certain relationship to this object? If we examine the same object with the aid of an instrument, for example a magnifying glass or a microscope, does it somehow change the relation of the observer to the object being observed?

Making allowance for possible further arguments to the above questions, it can be said that in fact descriptive propositions and valuational ones both express a certain relationship to reality. Yet descriptive propositions are not modified by the emotional attitude of the perceiving subject, whereas valuation is so modified. If someone says: 'Young persons are not fully formed members of the community,' an opinion takes the form of a descriptive proposition. On the other hand, if someone says: 'Young persons should not be punished as severely as adults'—he utters a valuational proposition. Undoubtedly, the former utterance is a description of a certain state of affairs (possibly based on various data obtained by research techniques), whereas the latter (which may—but need not—be based on such data obtained by research) contains also—besides any *implicit* cognitive content—the following valuation: 'It is a bad thing to punish young persons as severely as adults.' In his attempts to distinguish between descriptive and valuational propositions, Zygmunt Ziembiński notes a similar aspect: 'When we direct our attention to something, we not only state that it is so and so, we not only intellectually register facts, but we frequently assume an emotional attitude toward these, approving or disapproving of the fact that a given state of affairs took or will take place. Emotional attitudes of this kind toward events or a state of affairs, which are either the objects spoken about or products of imagining certain states or events, are called valuation.' And 'Valuation is a certain experience, i.e. it is an event in a person's mind.'[4] Can we in this connection generalize that description and valuation are both a certain relationship of the perceiving subject toward reality, description being characterized by the absence of emotional elements in the said relationship, whereas valuation is characterized by the presence of emotional elements? To answer this question further notional distinctions must be made.

Valuation 'proper' and valuation 'as to purposefulness' (utilitarian)

To say that breaking a contract is condemnable is—undoubtedly—a valuation. What does this valuation mean? It means that a person breaking a contract will be condemned in the circles in which this norm prevails. This kind of statement refers to facts: it anticipates that in a given milieu a person who does not adhere to contracts is recognized as such, and is penalized by being removed from lists of prospective customers, by social control, by commercial or social ostracism, etc. In other words, the statement says that if you do not want to experience unpleasant and painful consequences of this kind, you should not behave like that. To cite another example, there is the valuational proposition: 'Being a delator (informer) is morally wrong.' The valuation could assume a different form. It is well known that although a notorious delator may derive immediate profits from his activity, in the long run he will be recognized as a delator, socially isolated, condemned, and generally despised. Thus a certain behavioral pattern is accepted by seeing how other people evaluate it, as well as according to how it fits into one's existing value system.

If we define the valuation 'proper' as being the one according to which it is censurable to break a contract, or it is morally wrong to be a cheat, and if we define as utilitarian the statement that a person who does not want to incur repression should adhere to contracts, or if he does not want to be socially ostracized he should not delate, does it not seem likely that *the valuation 'proper' is a residuary, abridged, somewhat stunted form of utilitarian valuation*?

Let us note that such interpretation of the terms 'proper' and 'utilitarian' differs from the semantic analysis by Maria Ossowska. A thorough semantic analysis of various senses of the terms 'valuation proper' and 'utilitarian valuation' is to be found in a paper by Ossowska on the two kinds of valuation.[5] She discusses three basic proposals for distinguishing valuations proper from utilitarian valuations. According to the first, utilitarian valuations are statements predicating that a thing is suitable for some purpose, that it is good or useful. According to the second, 'utilitarian valuations refer to means, whereas valuations proper refer to ends.' The third interpretation 'links the notion of valuation proper with the so-called

THE NOTION OF VALUATION

intrinsic property of the thing . . . , and the notion of utilitarian valuation with the so-called extrinsic value of the thing. . . .' It could be generalized that valuations proper are—on the basis of semantic distinctions—valuations *par excellence*, whereas utilitarian valuations are derivative valuations, devoid of subjective elements.

Returning to the problem of the methodological nature of 'valuation proper,' the question should be asked whether such a statement as, for example, 'Being a delator is reprehensible' could be expressed by means of a utilitarian proposition. Could we say: 'If you do not want to meet—in spite of possible transitory profits—with permanent social contempt, do not be a cheater'? Such a utilitarian proposition tells us what is likely to happen (is predictable according to socially accumulated experience) and states that what will probably happen will be unpleasant, and—calculating profits and losses—it dissuades from certain behavior. Supposedly, this form of the utilitarian valuational proposition simultaneously reconstructs the negative process of internalization of the norm relating to prevention of denunciatory activities. Supposedly, the said process results in a more or less successful inculcation of the norm in a given community and its members. When this kind of internalization has been accomplished, the didactics of the utilitarian valuation can be given up as redundant, unwieldy in practice, and the valuation 'proper,' i.e. the residuary form of the utilitarian valuation with its sanction, reproof or condemnation, will take over. To avoid terminological confusion which might arise from the preceding application of the term 'utilitarian valuation' it will be helpful in our further discussion to call the basic valuation from which valuation 'proper' is derivable—the 'valuation as to purposefulness.'

The above conclusion, relating to the residuary nature of valuations 'proper,' if correct, would involve far-reaching theoretical and practical implications.

Consequences of valuations 'proper' being reduced to valuations 'as to purposefulness'

First of all it would appear that the unbridgeable gulf between descriptive propositions and valuational propositions is of a semantic nature (resulting from the comparison of two different semantic categories). The gulf is specified as semantic, because—after corresponding semantic transformations—it becomes an apparent gap. A complex dispute, dramatically breaking the gnoseological oneness of the world, would appear a controversy arising from comparing two different semantic categories. Valuations 'proper' should be treated (contrary to what the very name suggests—incidentally, the name being symptomatic of its very nature having been as yet unspecified) not as such, but as valuations non-proper. From the point of view of social practice, it is more expedient to use only the notion of acceptance or rejection as it is expressed by valuation, instead of a constant prognosis as to the purposefulness of one's behavior and its consequences.

We seem to have arrived at an answer to the question posed. Thus: is it really so that either description or valuation is a certain relationship between the perceiving subject and reality, valuation differing from description by the presence of emotional elements in valuation? The answer is: No, because the so-called valuation proper is in fact a dependent statement. It is part of a fuller utterance which is the valuation as to purposefulness. The emotional character of valuations which were treated as proper, the character which was to constitute their coherence and distinctness, is—as we have tried to show—a didactic operation of the social process which internalizes various norms. Consequently valuations 'proper' would be reducible to valuations as to purposefulness. On the other hand, no semantic difference is noticeable between the proposition valuational as to purposefulness and the purely descriptive propositions.

Yet when identifying propositions valuational as to purposefulness with descriptive propositions do we not offend well-established intuitions? Undoubtedly, we do. Nevertheless, the point is not to respect intuitions connected with meanings commonly attached to various terms, but to grasp relevant internal connections between phenomena. Although it might be said that the valuational proposition 'Fraud is bad behavior' is a specific element of the proposition valuational as to purposefulness, i.e. 'If you do not wish to be condemned, by all means do not abuse anybody's confidence,' the question arises whether we can state that the proposition valuational as to purposefulness is equivalent to a descriptive proposition: 'If you do not abuse other people's confidence, you will not be condemned on these grounds'. The answer is: Yes. Not to abuse confidence is socially a means of not giving rise to condemnation. The fact of not abusing confidence functionally depends on not giving rise to condemnation. In this case the valuation as to purposefulness is adapted to the requirements of practical life experience by imparting theoretical knowledge which registers special interdependences.

Valuations seem to be phenomena out of another world not only because they carry emotional loads instilled by internalization processes, but also because their linguistic structure, apparently different from that of descriptive propositions (which usually do not contain predicative words 'good' or 'bad,' approval or disapproval), is seemingly uniform, due to the presence of such normatively tinged expressions. Yet the illusion of such uniformity, suggested by a similar linguistic structure, would not persist, were it not for certain essential considerations, of both a linguistic and a gnoseological nature.

Thus an additional aspect is to be taken into account. Reality is reducible to three basic categories. Two basic categories proposed by T. Kotarbiński (as principal and exclusive) are—it seems—insufficient for some important considerations. Although it is essential —according to Kotarbiński—that reality consists of things and perceiving beings, yet certain regions of reality are not fully reducible to these two categories. Any conventions, agreements more or less consciously concluded, mutually accepted obligations, constitute an additional plane of reality which should be specifically distinguished. To express doubts we might say that agreements are merely certain emotional states of the persons affected. So they are. Yet, how can bilaterally consistent emotions, similar in some specific aspect, be fully explicable? How is this formal identity arrived at? How does an extremely orderly system of analogical coincidences arise? On what basis do similar, systematically arranged emotions emerge? The pacts mutually concluded—whatever their external manifestations— remain incomprehensible to a casual observer until he learns what contractual data have been incorporated by mutual agreement in corresponding duties and claims. No observation or linguistic interpretation will apprehend the underlying mutual agreement. Agreements of this kind form—after things and perceiving beings—the third dimension of reality. The establishment of a timetable binding on the railway stations in Moscow and Rome need not link the two cities with any human or material bonds. Any groups of passengers, parts of a given train, may be replaced on the way, and it may happen that no element present at one station (passenger, guard, luggage, carriage) will appear at the other station. Yet in spite of all the relevant elements being replaceable, one permanent feature remains. This is the convention concluded, expressed in relevant entries in railway timetables.

The world of mutual conventions, petrified in more or less coherent systems, gives rise to the belief in its own internal order. The fact that the systems have been created by numberless assays and errors, systematic corrections and adaptations, is disregarded unless these are of genetic interest. As a result a uniform order of elements, arranged conventionally, not naturalistically, emerges. This seemingly homogeneous order, disregarding the individual functional and instrumental purposes of its particular elements, provides data systematically to establish the belief that valuation is qualitatively different from description. The said belief makes it difficult to see the real character of valuations: their being informatory as to the appropriate means to specific ends.

It seems particularly useful to introduce, at this point, such notions as: categoric attitude and teleological attitude, ethics individually oriented and ethics socially oriented.

The categoric attitude may be defined as direct acceptance or rejection of a certain rule relating to behavior, whereas the teleological attitude is the attitude in which either acceptance or rejection of the behavior depends on specific reckonings, consideration of possible variants of behavior and evaluation of their consequences.

Investigations show that categoric attitudes can be distinguished, and that such attitudes are related to various ways to different—objective and subjective—social elements.

The teleological attitude is connected with the following elements: a person respectively younger, with a respectively higher education level. The categoric attitude, on the other hand, is conditioned by the fact of being respectively older with respectively lower education level. The symptoms of the feeling of insecurity and maladjustment are connected with the teleological attitude and are absent in the categoric attitude.

The relationship between a higher education level and the teleological attitude and a respectively lower education level and the categoric attitude is especially interesting. The said relationship seems to evidence that the development of personality proceeds, as a rule, by collecting and accumulating various intuitions, emotions, reactions, reflections, experience, and not by one-sided, calculative sharpening of reflexation. In any case, with increasing experience, the already internalized elements of categoric attitude turn into the teleological attitude.

We should, however, avoid oversimplifications. The teleological attitude is not 'bad,' and the categoric attitude is not 'good.' What concerns individuals need not be applicable to social groups or to social systems. A stabilized social system with categoric attitudes prevailing therein need not be 'good,' and an unstabilized social system with prevailing teleological attitudes need not be 'bad.' Generally speaking, a serious doubt arises whether valuations 'proper' can provide grounds for giving such judgments, and we wonder if the valuation as to purposefulness is not this kind of attitude.

Let us now indicate some possible applications of the concept of individually and socially oriented ethics.

The bourgeois ethic can be interpreted as an egoistic ethic (combining the teleological attitude and the tendency to safeguard one's own interests in the first place), turning toward the consumption of material goods. In contradistinction, the socially oriented can be interpreted as an altruistic ethic (combining the categoric attitude and the tendency to safeguard the interests of other people) turning toward overcoming injustice and attaining social justice. It seems that the bourgeois ethic can—in certain elements—be derived from the Christian ethic, as the latter concentrates its attention on direct (or such as can be direct) human relations in small groups—family, neighbors, friends. Being entangled in these direct relationships—if not counterbalanced by an adequate affiliation to supra-individual metaphysical ideals—inclines to seeing ethical phenomena narrowly. Within the 'face to face' ethic, attitudes and behavior are evaluated, the consequences of which are directly noticeable in the life of a certain small social group. Experience of this kind when it is summed up, makes it difficult—or even impossible—to perceive sometimes far-reaching consequences of performing particular social functions, or occupying certain social positions. 'Valuations proper' are the final product of the summing up.

Individually oriented ethics is an essential structural element of the Christian or bourgeois ethic, as it emphasizes a predisposition toward a certain individual and the evaluation of this individual according to socially and directly observable results of his activity. In contradistinction, the socially oriented ethic, as it expresses its judgment after the detection and analysis of what is sometimes a long sequence of consequences, following a seemingly neutral position being occupied or an ethically apparently neutral role being played, and functioning within an apparently morally neutral social system, evaluates finally the global outcome of the scrutinized action. By developing the system of valuations as to purposefulness we could reveal whether certain social relations—seemingly exempt from being morally evaluated—are functional or not, or amend the existing valuations.

When discussing further possible implications of the viewpoint concerning the nature of valuations, it seems expedient to devote a few words to the problem of distinguishing moral and aesthetic valuations, a typical example of a theoretically barren set of problems. An opinion is held that aesthetic valuations are valuations 'proper.' Maria Ossowska says that this opinion should be reviewed, though she does not expound this problem. According to her, when valuating aesthetically one tends to isolate the object being evaluated from its environment, which is not the case with moral valuation.[6]

What is the nature of this problem in view of the conception outlined? If we say that valuations proper are apparent valuations (and they are such because their instrumental sense either has not been recognized, or has been intentionally camouflaged), the said thesis applies both to moral and aesthetic valuations. Nevertheless, in the case of a moral judgment approval or disapproval refers, first of all, to human relations, with the sanity of social relations in view— hence the tendency to put moral norms into a context which is broader than the subject being evaluated; whereas instrumental aesthetic valuations ('egoistically') refer, first and foremost, to the evaluating subject—hence the tendency to isolate the object being evaluated from a broader context. The valuational proposition 'This flower is beautiful' in fact states that the sensory impression evoked by the flower is a proper means to the emotional satisfaction of the evaluating person.

Conclusions

The above leads us to at least three main conclusions.[7] First, doubts arise as to the veracity of the thesis about the methodological autonomy of valuations. We are inclined to suspect that a certain 'proper' or emotional valuation—irrespective of what it says—has also a teleological sense more essential than its content, the said sense making it necessary to treat the valuation as an instrumental means to purposes which are not always explicitly set out. The opinions, attitudes or behavior, awarded or punished with valuations, are—according to this conception—symptoms arrived at according to certain mechanisms, adaptations, evolution, integration, reintegration, or disintegration of various elements in a given social system. Consequently, to understand what a given valuation means, we have to 'take the gilt off' it and establish what functions it actually performs.

Second, new—after having accepted this viewpoint—and broad prospects will open to normative legal sciences. New potential possibilities will open when the said sciences—imbued with valuations 'proper' of various kinds and permeated with them to such a degree that they form a quasi-autonomous world—fully realize (through their representatives) the apparent character of valuations 'proper' and their real nature as valuations as to purposefulness. Such possibilities arise because it will be a methodological duty of particular normative disciplines to look for aims which individual valuations as to purposefulness (in the form of regulations) serve and to establish to what extent the valuations are instrumentally efficient in justifying any steps to this end. The main task of legal sciences, which is the problem of the efficacy of law, will then gain grounds for empirical—and practical—implementation.

Third, the introduction of such notions as the attitude as to purposefulness, principal attitude, individually and socially oriented ethics, to the discussion of Man in general, not to ethical discussions, shows that the variety of problems pertaining to the Arts is much greater than it was ever thought. It also provides cognitive instruments critically to reveal defects of the traditional way of thinking. The thinking in the categories of valuations as to purposefulness may disclose that certain domains of human relations, seemingly not liable to valuation 'proper,' are by no means ethically neutral. As a result it enables the scope of ethical judgment to be extended and provides grounds for revaluing ethical judgments established in close circles, and also for showing their possible inadequacy when applied to social macrostructures. Naturally, care should be taken not to have these cognitive instruments of higher precision used to create more subtle ethical mystifications.

Obviously, the above conclusions, as well as the preceding discourse, are controversial in relation to the hitherto existing views. In this connection let us hope that eventual discussion will reveal its possible faults and merits.

It would be too hasty to judge the above-mentioned considerations as too remote from the main topic of the present analysis, which is the unique characteristics of practical social sciences. The traditional social sciences accumulated several contradictions which should not be omitted or neglected. (1) Theoretical social sciences are quite well developed but their social futility is well recognized. On the other hand practical social sciences are underdeveloped but the need to utilize them is quite strong. (2) The distinction between 'is' and 'ought to be' is regarded as the essential feature of social sciences or as a mischievious methodological and political trap. Consequently there is a tendency to expel all value statements from the language of social sciences or to treat all statements of social sciences as loaded by invisible but hidden values. (3) Despite these existing discrepancies the need for the unity of social sciences is quite visible as a methodological postulate, or as the perception of social reality. (4) Politization of social sciences seems to be an easy solution but it contradicts the universal postulate of sciences; its intersubjective, informative and testing functions.

Taking these antinomies into consideration, the Introduction attempted to solve those contradictions by reducing the gap between the notions of values and descriptive statements in order to propose the unified conceptual scheme which might be adequate for the solution of the problem of practical social sciences.

2 What is the concern of the practical sciences?

According to Petrażycki, and to Lande who developed Petrażycki's idea, the practical sciences 'speak about what ought to be; they express rules of conduct.'[1] According to T. Kotarbiński, a practical science is a discipline dealing chiefly with designs or projects.[2]

The former definition is too broad. For the practical sciences do not speak about what ought to be; they teach how the goals approved by accepted values can be attained. What ought to be is the subject of various systems of evaluative propositions which are accepted in extra-scientific ways. However, this definition is not completely pointless, for some rules of conduct, the purposive ones, are in fact a subject-matter of the practical sciences.

The second definition is more to the point. To say that the practical sciences deal with projects is sound inasmuch as they point to the means permitting attainment of what ought to be, and this they can only do by suggesting projects of action. However, projects can be accepted or rejected. The practical sciences are interested in what makes some projects acceptable and others not. Acceptance or rejection of projects seems to depend on the established system of values. Thus defining the practical sciences as those which undertake projects, even though this is certainly one of their most remarkable features, would leave out the problem of evaluations, which seems to be the essential one.[3]

To coordinate our main themes, we can say that neither the attitude of the practical sciences in respect to the future nor their attitude in respect to the descriptive propositions are their distinguishing characteristics. For the practical sciences are based, on the one hand, on accepted evaluations, i.e. on value judgments, and on the other on established relationships of facts. The accepted evaluations concern the approved states of affairs and define objectives which are thought desirable to be attained. The relationships between facts inform as to what means and factors have to be made use of in order to attain the objectives. Thus, the practical sciences involve both the elements of evaluation and of description. This point must be stressed, for it is only a conjunction of evaluation and description that can determine action.

Utterances of the practical sciences are utilitarian judgments. They connect in a peculiar manner evaluation and description. For example: 'In order to secure efficient functioning of a legal system, an optimal compromise must be found between its uniformity, involving the usage of the special consistent legal language, and its comprehensibility for those to whom it is addressed.' This utilitarian judgment entails a value judgment proper and a descriptive proposition. The value judgment is an approval of the opinion that legal systems ought to function efficiently; the description expounds the postulates of uniformity and of comprehensibility of legal systems. In fact, these postulates define necessary but not sufficient conditions of efficiency of legal systems.

Thus, a characteristic feature of the practical sciences is their attitude to evaluations as determinants of action.

In relation to the problem of the criterion for distinguishing between the theoretical and practical disciplines, some remarks on evaluation seem necessary. The theoretical sciences do not use value judgments as their essential propositions. In their study of reality they produce descriptive or analytic statements and tend to eliminate evaluations as far as possible from their discourse. The practical disciplines do use evaluations, but their role within the practical discourse is quite peculiar.

Propositions like 'human life should be protected' or 'it would be good if human life was protected' are evaluations. But the proposition: 'in a given historical period and society, the death penalty serves to protect human life on a large scale,' is a theoretical descriptive proposition (either true or false).

Established evaluative systems will contain evaluative types of propositions. A third type belongs to the subject-matter of a theoretical science, sociology. A practical science, legal policy in this case, attempts to integrate evaluations and descriptions into a peculiar semantical whole. The integration is established by connecting evaluation with description by means of the conjunctive phrases 'if—then' or 'in order to—it should.' In our example, the conjunction will be made by stating that 'in a given historical period and society, in order to protect human life on a large scale, the death penalty should be applied.' In accord with our earlier definitions, a proposition built in this manner is called a utilitarian judgment. It is a correct proposition if the descriptive statement on which it is based is true, and if the evaluation contained in it has been accepted; it is a faulty proposition if either the descriptive proposition is false, or the evaluation has failed to be accepted.

It follows from this that the practical sciences consist of utilitarian judgments. They are marked by the condition that they unite evaluative and descriptive elements. However, the union is of a distinctive character. For the practical disciplines are not concerned with the validity or wrongness of the evaluations which are included in their purposive propositions. The evaluations have been brought to them as a challenge, and what the practical sciences are expected to do is to find the best means to attain the objectives presented in the evaluations, and by no means to call them into doubt. The practical sciences can be based on any system of values. Their sole task is to find means to realize these values, whatever they may be. This does not mean that the goals which the practical sciences have to help in attaining, or the means suggested by practical sciences, should not be evaluated; to the contrary, such an evaluation of ends and means seems to be indispensable, but this goes beyond the boundaries of the practical sciences themselves.

An analogy can be made between the role of the practical sciences and, for example, the job of a tailor. The tailor can cut garments for priests, rascals, scientists, dogs, etc. If he undertakes to make a suit, he ought to do it according to the best rules of his craft, independent of his liking or disliking his customer. The tailor can indeed refuse to make garments for rascals, and such a declaration will influence his activity. However, he would be a poor craftsman if he expressed his dislike for rascals in careless work.

The following definition of the practical disciplines can be proposed. The practical sciences are aggregates of general propositions, stating how the states of affairs recommended by the accepted evaluations can be realized by making use of established factual regularities. Examples of the practical sciences are medicine, architecture, the policy of law, pedagogics, agricultural disciplines, trade disciplines, various branches of technology, etc.

Summing up the considerations on the criteria of distinction between the practical and theoretical disciplines, we can say that the practical disciplines are marked by a definite position with respect to evaluations and action. The practical disciplines take into account, without calling them into doubt, only those evaluations which require that definite actions be recommended.

3 The practical natural sciences and the practical social sciences

The practical disciplines are preoccupied with inventing procedures for attaining the desired, and only the desired, states of affairs. They can be divided into two kinds.

To the first kind belong such disciplines as pedagogics, social policy, legal policy, psychotherapy, economic policy, etc. These are concerned with how to attain certain states of affairs which have been positively valued for individual or social reasons. In these disciplines the problem of evaluations—their multiplicity, incompatibility and various emotional backgrounds—plays a particularly important role. These disciplines have their counterparts among the theoretical sciences, such as psychology, sociology, theory of law, psychiatry, economics.

To the second type belong such disciplines as architecture, medicine, mechanics, agronomy, etc. These are preoccupied with inventing exact procedures for attaining certain states of affairs evaluated to be desirable, but the emphasis is on the technical aspect of the relevant activities, rather than on the acceptance of some values rather than others.

Essentially, the practical procedures in the social and natural sciences are the same, for the principle of effectiveness is preeminent in both. Nevertheless there are differences between these two types of the practical disciplines. In the first place, as just noted, in the practical social sciences the problem of values and judgments elicits more attention, while in the practical natural disciplines it is the development of techniques and manipulations which tends to predominate. But a more detailed elaboration and comparison of the modes of practical endeavors is needed in order to establish the common and the discrepant features of the natural and social disciplines. In the present work we want to consider the general characteristics of the practical sciences of both types, but with a particular emphasis on the social disciplines. In trying to grasp some of the general differences between them, we can observe the following:

Game and decision theorists emphasize that uncertainty and risk are a greater burden in the applied social disciplines than in the other applied sciences, and thus it is more difficult to build projects on the basis of data supplied by the social sciences.

Four further differences are pointed to by R. K. Merton. These are connected with the fact that it is intellectuals (as opposed to technicians) who are engaged in applying the practical social sciences.[1] Thus, to begin with, the relationships between experts and their clients are indefinite, for the identification of an expert is rather difficult and is usually a consequence of the assumption that a respectable position (as with a university) implies competence. Second, experts choose other experts on a personal rather than a competency basis, and thus deviations from sound knowledge can result from interpersonal relations. A third difference is related to the fact that the practical social sciences are engaged in activity, and those who make the decisions often believe that their first-hand knowledge originating in experience is more reliable than what the experts can offer them. Finally, intellectuals engaged in the applied social sciences are vulnerable to attacks by those who may see the results of researches as being unfavorable for them; in such an insecure situation intellectuals may be apt to produce biased results.

To this list we can add another peculiarity. In applied social sciences, besides knowledge and researches, an approval of the intended objectives is necessary. Thus, in those sciences there must be an alliance of neutral knowledge and evaluative decisions. In the course of a practical enterprise the evaluations will be taken for granted and no longer disputed, but for it to be undertaken at all these evaluative decisions must be made.

In the applied natural sciences the situation is different. Utilitarian judgments are implied in them at every moment, but only in exceptional cases are evaluative judgments at stake. When a model car is designed, such elements as its weight, speed, size, quality of the engine, shape, etc., are projected and appreciated (in utilitarian judgments) from the point of view of their utility in this particular type of car. There is no room here for value judgments proper. These appear only in relatively rare situations, by no means typical for the natural applied sciences, as when a scientist must face the task of designing a gas chamber for mass murder or a deadly ballistic missile.

part two

A description of the practical social sciences

4 The course of purposive procedure

The basic element of the practical sciences is the course of purposive procedures. The concept of a purposive procedure is broader than the concept of purposive reasoning. It includes both purposive reasoning and the action leading to the realization of the assumed purposes.

The course of purposive procedure can be analyzed into several interdependent links, which must be distinguished as follows: diagnosis, including the phases of description, comparison of evaluations, conclusion, explanation, and postulative suggestions and hypotheses; justification; project building; realization of the project; control and judgment of results. Purposive reasoning has the following phases: diagnosis and its elements; justification; some of the elements of project building; some of the elements of control; judgment.

There is a certain essential difference between the logical rules of sound reasoning and the rules of a correct course of purposive procedure. For while a violation of any rule of correct logical reasoning must inevitably lead to an error, a violation of the rules of valid purposive procedure can, but need not, lead to a practical fallacy.

If we accept T. Kotarbiński's definition of the practical error,[1] we can see that a violation of the rules of correct purposive procedure can lead to performance of a futile or dysfunctional activity. I shall try to present some of the directives and conditions of sound purposive procedure after an analysis of its several elements.

At any rate, the paramount challenge of the practical disciplines is the transformation of reality. Their main task is to teach how a cycle of actions and reasonings can make two states of affairs compatible. The first one is imagined, postulated and described by a project; the other one is realized. If as a consequence of a purposive procedure these two states of affairs are made compatible, then it can be said that the obtained results are in agreement with the suggested project and that the course of purposive action has been correct. If there is no such compatibility, it means either that the project has failed to be realized (futile actions have been carried out) or that although it has been realized a state of affairs has been obtained which has not been intended (dysfunctional activities have been carried out). Frequently, in order to attain the intended ends an agent of action will undertake actions to improve on the so far unsatisfactory results.

Example

The third method succeeded. Belfort. Mrs Rousselle, 32, mother of two children, definitely wanted to put an end to her life. At first she tried to stab herself with a knife. When this method failed, the desperate woman put a rope around her neck and tried to hang herself. This failed, too. Then the miserable woman stepped into a tub full of water and turned on the gas. This time death came and did its job. Mrs Rousselle left a letter announcing her intention to commit suicide.

Though this case does not belong to any practical discipline, and does not necessarily present an example of good taste, it is nevertheless rather remarkable.[2]

The diagnosis

A diagnosis is the first link in the chain of purposive procedure. It consists of the following five interdependent, basic, phases: description, evaluation, conclusion, explanation, and postulating or proposing of hypotheses.

By description is meant a listing of all recorded empirical data toward which purposive action will eventually be directed. By evaluation is meant a listing of all the value judgments that can be relevant to the empirical data. Conclusion is the phase of purposive procedure in which a need (or its lack) for further purposive action is stated by applying the system of accepted judgments to the described states of reality. The next element of diagnosis is explanation, genetic and causal, of the states of affairs which are to be realized, transformed, or removed. The last phase of the diagnosis is acceptance of a hypothesis, assuming a causal relationship between the project considered as a result and some factor supposed to be its cause. Thus we can define diagnosis as the formulation of a hypothesis for the changing of actual states of affairs, established by complete description and evaluation of empirical situations.

Moreover, a broader and a narrower meaning of diagnosis must be distinguished. In the narrower sense diagnosis covers description, evaluation and evaluative conclusion; in the broader sense it includes, besides, explanation and the postulating or building of hypotheses. A similar distinction is accepted in the methodology of theoretical sciences, although the problem of evaluation, important for the practical disciplines, is omitted.

TABLE 1

White jobs	Workers in these jobs in 1940 who were white %	Negro jobs	Workers in these jobs in 1940 who were Negro %
		Men	
Boilermakers	100	Charmen, janitors, porters	92
Motormen	99	Laborers, utilities	91
Telegraph operators	99	Laborers, construction	80
Bookkeepers and accountants	99	Servants	77
Conductors	99	Laborers, manufacturing	76
Machinists	98	Elevator operators	74
Telegraph, telephone linemen	98	Laborers, trade	72
		Laborers, railroad	71
Metalworkers	97	Cooks	68
Printing craftsmen	96	Laundry operatives	60
		Messengers	57
		Women	
Stenographers, typists	99	Elevator oporators	89
Telephone operators	98	Cooks	85
Clerical workers	97	Charwomen	82
Librarians	96	Servants	78

Example. Table 1, made from data contained in a report by the National Committee on Racial Segregation in Washington, D.C., consists of descriptive data only and does not offer any suggestions concerning the means of change. It illustrates only that part of the diagnosis which is a record of the empirically available data.[3]

It can thus be seen that here the meaning of diagnosis is different from the common usage. Usually we see the essential feature of diagnosis, as suggested chiefly by medical usage, to be that it offers a hypothesis explaining why some undesirable situations or conditions actually occur. In medicine the term 'diagnosis' is used when the symptoms observed in a patient are consistent with those that are typical for a specific disease.

Example. The syndrome of weakness, emaciation, peculiar yellowness of skin, stomach pains, can lead to suspicion of a tumor or cancer of the stomach. A surgical and histopathological finding of cancerous cells in the tumor imposes the diagnosis: 'cancer.' This means that the present symptoms have been subsumed under the more general proposition describing characteristic symptoms. Using this kind of diagnosis, i.e. an identification of the particular type of disease, a physician is able to prescribe a therapy even if he does not know the causes of the disease, as in the case of cancer, because he can resort to the accumulated experience of the profession. His procedure is the following: after finding the symptoms which are typical for some definite disease, the case is identified accordingly and practical prescriptions are administered which seem to be appropriate.

Thus, a medical diagnosis is the identification of a disease on the ground of the present symptoms. In the applied social sciences such a procedure is not feasible. Medicine is preoccupied with deviations in the functioning of an organism, for which it is relatively easy to define the normal state; however, it is rather difficult to tell what is the normal course of social processes. Due to complex and unique situations and to the narrow range of experience, there are no definite 'diagnostic units' or remedies in the social sciences which are highly specific and well tested.

Thus the concept of diagnosis in the broader sense attempts to include in a single whole all those phases of the purposive procedure which are indispensable for a proper description of the studied situation, for an understanding of the factors influencing it, and for pointing to the means for changing the situation if this is necessary. Such a concept of diagnosis seems to fit better the intuitions of the social sciences, in which diagnostics would cover not only a sufficient recognition of the facts and an analysis of their causes, but also the pointing to the means for their improvement.

Description. By description of the observed states of affairs we shall mean recording of facts in empirical terms, appropriate in the given field of knowledge. A description ought to be exhaustive and clear, and it should order the material by means of classifications. Besides, a description ought to be generalized by referring to the laws governing the development of what actually is the fact and to the causes explaining its origin.

In all sciences, and thus also in the applied social sciences, as for example in the policy of law, the description ought to be made in terms which are appropriate to the given discipline. The point is that there is room here for introducing into the practical sciences the research methods, and in particular the methods of collecting data, employed in various social sciences. The methods of demography, statistics, economics, sociography, are useful for the respective practical disciplines. The methods of data collecting can be very different, from the most general investigations of mass phenomena by means of questionnaires, interviews and the other sociographic methods, to the most individualized techniques. These methods can be applied for various ends and they can be introduced in multiple ways.

Evaluations. The set of evaluations by means of which the described states of affairs can be judged refers to that set which is accepted in the given purposive procedure, and so ordered that all the evaluations that can be relevant to the given states of affairs are stated and hierarchically arranged. The hierarchical arrangement of judgments ought to be such that if discrepant judgments appear, general directives will be handy to determine the validity of individual judgments and to establish the final evaluation. As the set or catalogue of evaluations includes all the evaluations accepted during a purposive procedure, we have to insert into it not only the positive but also the negative judgments, or those which establish a limitation for action and shed light upon the discrepancy between the available means and the desired ends.[4]

The problem of evaluation is significantly related to the problem of description. The central dilemma in the latter is: How can an exhaustive description of some states of affairs be attempted if we do not know in advance which of their features ought to be analyzed, and to what extent? For the objective phenomena are characterized by an immense multitude of features and only some of them can be recorded, even if the description is the most meticulous and systematic. The question is, then, which of them should be attended to?

The accepted value judgments not only contain the elements of approval or disapproval,[5] they also state what the evaluations refer to, for they usually contain a description of the evaluated state of affairs. The positive judgments describe the postulated states of affairs, and the negative judgments describe the states of affairs which are disapproved. And here we find the key to solving the problem of the extent to which a state of affairs should be described. It can be described from the point of view of the accepted evaluations. This can be done by comparing the existing state of affairs with both the postulated and the undesirable ones. Since the postulated states of affairs—i.e. those which have been positively evaluated and toward which a decision to realize them has been taken—are the objectives of activity, then we can say that it is the objectives of that activity which determine the scope of description. In a way, then, evaluation takes primacy over descriptive cognition. The essential risk of a practical activity is that its description is determined by its objectives. The risk is in the extent to which the objectives have not been properly chosen. If some relevant evaluations turn out not to have been included in the objectives, then the fact that they have been omitted may make some trouble, but only some time after the practical activity has been undertaken or even completed.

As in the phase of description various methods can be used for data collecting, so are there relevant techniques for collecting evaluative opinions. Again, sociographic methods play a particularly significant role in applied social sciences.

Example. The book by J. Cohen, R. A. H. Robson and A. Bates, *Parental Authority: The Community and the Law*,[6] can serve as an example of a work in which emotional evaluations and opinions in the realm of human interrelations called parental authority were collected, both for research purposes and for eventual projects *de lege ferenda*. In the study, 860 respondents, randomly sampled (one respondent for each 1,000 adult inhabitants of the State of Nebraska), were interviewed. One of the main assumptions of the study was defined as follows:[7]

> For the purposes of our undertaking, however, it is our position that *if* the moral sense of the community is relevant to the law-making process, either as a norm for the law-maker to consider, or as a norm to follow, it need not be left wholly to conjecture, to hunch or to intuition; and that modern social science techniques could more reliably be utilized for the task. . . .
> From a strictly 'if-then' vantage point, we merely suggest that *if* legal theorists and legislative and judicial law-makers *choose* to regard the moral sense of the community as a significant factor in the law-making process, it would seem incumbent upon them to obtain as reliable an estimate of this empirical fact as is possible—no matter how or to what extent it would be utilized in any particular formulation of law or theory of justice. Otherwise they would be subject to error.

Using specialized research techniques the authors arrive at a few general conclusions and many detailed ones. For example:[8]

> Parental authority is regarded as a means to an end, and there is little hesitance to employ the arm of the law to curb it when its exercise is perceived as being detrimental to the welfare of the child. There is comparatively little sentiment against the intrusion of law or government in what has, for so long a time,

been considered the private domain of the family; there is considerable feeling in favor of increased autonomy for the child—especially for the older child.

There are also other, more detailed conclusions. For example, opinions of respondents on some issues were compared with legal regulations on those issues. It turned out that in many cases there were essential discrepancies between what people believed and what the law prescribed. Tables 2 and 3 illustrate these conclusions.

TABLE 2[9] *Should a child have legal claims against his parents for parental wrongs to the child? (Expressed in percentages of total population.)*

Question		Yes	No	Don't know
25A	For negligent physical injury	47·6	44·4	8·0
25B	For negligent loss of child's money	72·9	22·9	4·2
25C	For theft of child's money	90·8	6·0	3·1
25D	For seduction of child	89·5	6·5	4·0

TABLE 3[10] *Child's legal claims against his parents for parental wrongs to the child: comparison of the law and the majority views of the community*

Question		Should child have legal claims against parents?	
		Law	Population
25A	For negligent physical injury	No	Evenly divided
25B	For negligent loss of child's money	Yes	Yes
25C	For theft of child's money	Yes	Yes
25D	For seduction of child	No	Yes

If the description and the evaluation are labeled initial steps in the diagnosis, their consequences can be quite varied.

(a) It can happen that matters as they stand are judged to be in accord with the accepted set of evaluations. In such case the final judgment is positive and there is no ground for undertaking a purposive procedure aiming at a change of the existing state of affairs. However, sometimes such a positive evaluation of all the relevant facts does not exclude the possibility of something better being attained. If such were the case and the positive judgment during the initial phase of the diagnosis was equivalent to a final decision to give up purposive action, then the process of improvement would be made impossible. However, this is actually not quite so, for it is the overall general evaluation which determines an undertaking of purposive action. It only comes about as a result of an evaluation of the projected action aiming at a change of the situation. Such an overall evaluation will be negative if, although the actual state can be improved, the change will be more expensive than tolerating the present shortcomings. For example, it was obvious some time ago that the Polish penal code of 1932 was not perfect, if only because of the changed social and economic situation after the Second World War. But consultation on the project of a novel penal code showed that a premature and hasty substitution of a new penal code for the old one would cost more than the consequences of the shortcomings of the old code. Eventually, a new penal code was introduced in 1970.

Thus, an initial diagnosis consists of a description of what is, and a conclusion as to whether it should or should not be changed. A prognosis of the costs of a change of the existing states of affairs is the necessary condition for reaching a conclusion.

(b) If all the described facts are negatively evaluated from the point of view of the accepted standards of value, a need for purposive action aiming at change may or may not arise. For a wholly negative judgment does not in all cases indicate a necessity to change the existing state of affairs. In extreme cases it can even happen that in spite of a fully negative initial diagnosis, purposive action will not have to be undertaken at all, or may be discontinued. This occurs when it is judged to be better to suffer the existing evil than to risk a greater evil as a result of the change. If, for example, repeated drillings fail to strike oil, then either the depth or the location or the method of drilling can be changed. In such case a negative result of a trial conduces to further efforts. But the negative result could lead as well to abandoning drilling in this particular region in spite of the conjecture that there is oil there, inasmuch as the drilling itself could be damaging beyond the prospects of gain. Thus a wholly negative evaluation can lead, contrary to expectations, to giving up some purposive action. However, the foregoing is a peculiar case: here the conclusion concerning the actual state would recommend corrective action, but the overall evaluation, including consideration of the purposive procedure itself, recommends giving it up entirely.

(c) In practice, the most frequent outcome is that some of the existing circumstances are appreciated positively and others negatively. In such a situation it is necessary to formulate the conclusion in accordance with the accepted values and their relative importance. By and large, if the conclusion is negative, purposive action should be undertaken; if it is positive, the project should not be undertaken.

However, the overall evaluation will often depend on how the effect of purposive action will be appreciated. It depends upon a prognosis of the overall effects. For it can happen that an undertaking of the purposive procedure will in itself—in its timing, organization and continuation, even though it would change the negative circumstances into positive ones—be so negatively appreciated that its positive results will be canceled. It was, for example, discovered that if litter straw is illuminated with green light, cows produce more milk. But installation of green lighting in a barn would cost more than the eventual dividend of milk.[11]

(d) Another type of relationship between description and evaluation in initial diagnosis is that wherein some positively evaluated circumstances are found to be lacking. For example, law-makers can discover that the legislation they have enacted has failed to bring about the intended positive effects. A finding that the positively evaluated state of affairs is lacking, together with a negative evaluation of such a lack can sometimes be sufficient ground for a negative evaluation of the whole enterprise. This case is different from those described above in that there it was actually existing states of affairs that were evaluated, whereas here it is the failure to achieve positive results that is subject to judgment.

Example. Research was undertaken on the effectiveness of sanitary regulations in the State of Nebraska.[12] In the course of that research, barbers were asked the following questions:

1 How often do you sterilize your instruments?
2 Do you use a sterilizing liquid? If yes, what liquid?
3 If you use a liquid, is it in any way hard on your instruments?
4 If you do not use liquids, what do you use?

A point was made of observing if the tools were kept in an enclosed cabinet when not in use, and if not, where they were kept.

The final task on the list was to try to keep a note of any comment the barbers had on the law as it now exists.

The results of the survey were rather shocking when one is aware of the possible diseases that can be passed on in a barber's shop. The fact was pointed up continually that most barbers do not feel their instruments can spread diseases and that, if they do at all, it is in a rare case. They apparently feel no obligation to stop those rare cases.

The results reduced to percentages are as follows:

	%
1 Violated the law in whole or in part	100
2 Liquids used to sterilize instruments	
(a) Soap and water	50
(b) Statutory liquids	$33\frac{1}{3}$
(c) Other commercial liquids	$16\frac{2}{3}$

3 How often the liquids are used
  (a) Once a day   44½
  (b) After each customer who looks diseased   50
  (c) When the barber thinks they need it   5½
4 Barbers who felt that razors need special care   39
5 Barbers who kept their tools in an enclosed
  cabinet   12

These results show beyond the slightest doubt that the law is being violated and in some cases is being completely ignored. The survey was difficult to tabulate completely because many of the barbers did sterilize the razors but completely ignored their clippers and scissors. They would clean their scissors once every two or three days.

While the law requires that the instruments be sterilized after each customer, the very best shop found only changed instruments after every four or five customers. The barbers all seem to feel that they run a clean shop and that no skin disease is ever spread through their tools.

Generally speaking, the research pointed to the lack of a certain state of affairs—namely, of the activities required by the regulations—and it was this lack which led to a negative evaluation of the existing situation.

(e) The preceding instances (a, b, c, d) are marked by the characteristic that certain states of affairs are evaluated from the point of view of the accepted value judgments and that the accepted system of evaluations provide the ground for an unambiguous appreciation of those states of affairs. That is to say, the described facts are appreciated either positively or negatively. However, the initial diagnosis may work differently. It can happen that facts are positively evaluated according to judgments belonging to one system of evaluations and at the same time are negatively evaluated in terms of a different system: this can be the case with all or some of the relevant facts. In such case, the undertaking (or the rejection) of a purposive action can be at the same time desirable and undesirable, depending on which of the incompatible systems of evaluations is referred to. In this kind of situation strategic decisions must be taken in order to avoid serious practical errors.

The above considerations (a) to (e) can be presented in the form of a diagram (see Figure 1).

As already noted, a negative evaluation of an existing state of affairs is a necessary condition for the undertaking of a purposive action, but it is not a sufficient condition. For the undertaking of a purposive action to be methodologically sound, two important factors must coincide. The first is a negative appreciation of the existing state of affairs, the other is a prognostic evaluation of a special kind. Such an evaluation must take into account the possible negative effects of the eventual purposive action, and it must assess whether these are lesser or greater than the negative effects of the existing circumstances. An undertaking of purposive action is sound only if it can be demonstrated that the negative effects of the existing state of affairs exceed the negative effects likely to be brought about by the projected change. It is popularly said, when some undesirable state of affairs is not eliminated because of the costs, that 'the skin is not worth the bark.' A comparison between

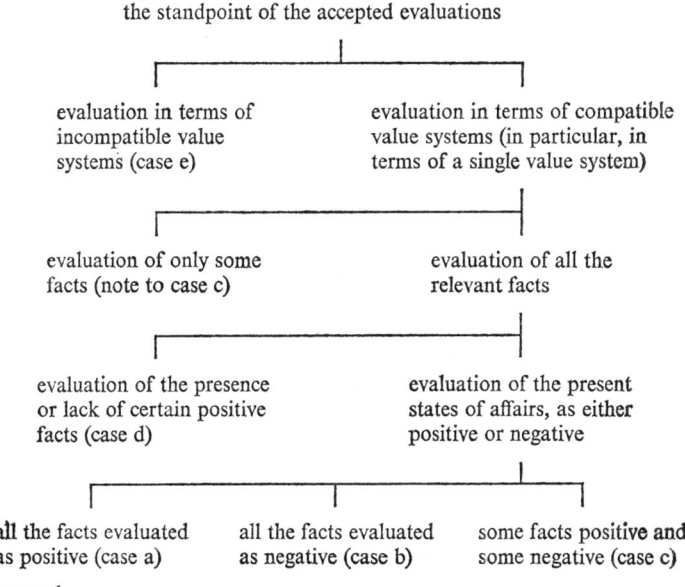

FIGURE 1

the negative effects of the existing circumstances and the probable negative effects of the course of purposive action itself yields what can be called the overall evaluation. If this is positive, it is thereby assumed that the eventual negative effects of the course of purposive action are lesser than the negative effects of tolerating the existing state of affairs. If the overall evaluation is negative, the situation is, of course, reversed. Thus it can be said that the sufficient condition for a purposive action to be undertaken is a negative evaluation of the existing circumstances and a positive overall evaluation. Therefore, in order to decide whether an action should be undertaken or rejected, it is necessary to step beyond the initial diagnosis in order to arrive at an overall evaluation.

Conclusions. Considering the essential consequences of the initial diagnoses, we may say that they can lead to one of three basic types of conclusions.

(1) Finding that there are negative effects in existing circumstances that can point to the necessity of undertaking some purposive action, either corrective or preventive. A corrective procedure has as its objective a change in the actual state of affairs resulting from a previous purposive action. The change may consist in substituting something else for what is, or in simply eliminating that which is. To use very simple examples, it can be said that a corrective procedure takes place when the yellow hue of a wall is negatively appreciated and the wall is repainted in blue, or when the dirt in a room becomes obnoxious and is cleaned up. Thus a corrective procedure consists not only in a negative appreciation of what is and in declaring that a change is necessary, but also in discovering the causes of the negative state of affairs and eliminating them, rendering them harmless, or substituting other things for them.

Example. A more complex corrective procedure can be illustrated by changes of traffic regulations.[13]

> Suggested changes in the law as a result of the jural laws, or the so-called warrants, have become commonplace in the art of controlling urban and rural traffic. Hundreds of changes are made in individual regulations every month to correspond with the results of studies. Stop signs, traffic lights, one-way streets, parking areas and right and left turns are constantly being altered to bring the control of traffic into better correspondence with jural laws involved and to improve control where warrants indicate a more effective operation.
>
> Figure 2 illustrates the results of such technique. At the crossing of U.S. 30 and the state highway pictured, because of a number of accidents, the city installed a set of automatic traffic lights where the traffic was far below the warranted volume. As a result, accidents actually increased. The state highway department made a study and suggested that the stop lights be replaced by a 'Stop Ahead' and a 'Stop' sign on the state highway on each side of U.S. 30. The result was a decrease in accidents from fourteen to one over similar periods before and after the change. The converging arrows on the illustration indicate the position and direction of the cars involved in the accidents.

In order to arrive at the conclusion that there are negative effects, the accepted valuations must be compared with the descriptive propositions recorded in that phase of description. If the record is incompatible with what is positively appreciated, the existing state

THE COURSE OF PURPOSIVE PROCEDURE

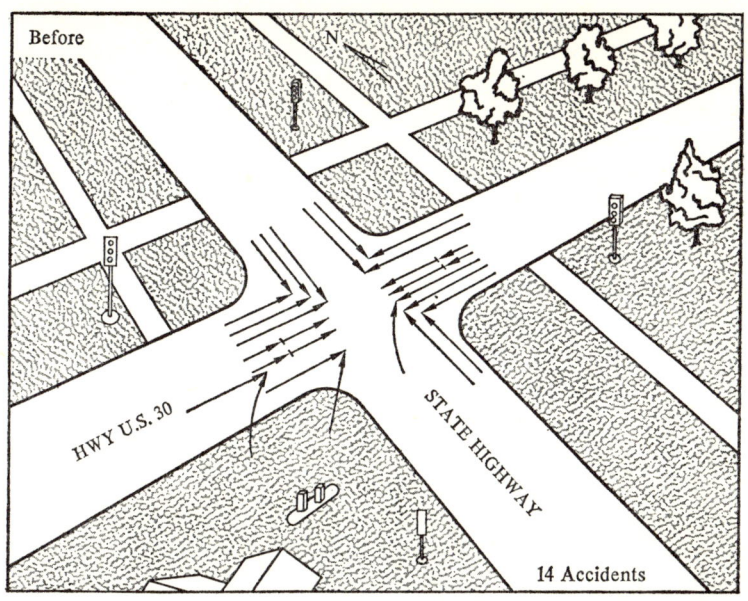

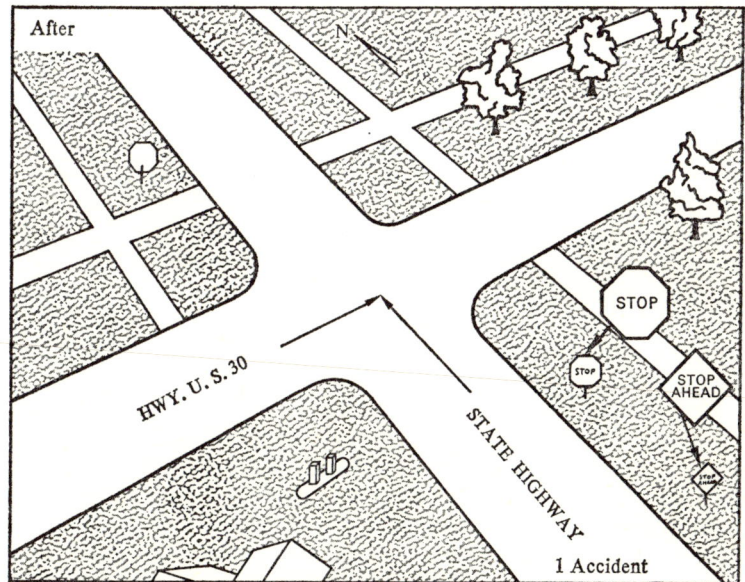

FIGURE 2 *The effect of an unwarranted traffic 'stop' & go signal. Accident experience two years before and after removal of signal*

of affairs must be negatively evaluated. For example, if it is appreciated that it would be good if during a definite time t the production of some product n increased up to or above the index i, and if it is ascertained in the course of description that the relevant increase of production of n during t was below i, then there is a discrepancy between the existing and the postulated state of affairs and, accordingly, production of n during t must be negatively appreciated.

Hence negatively appreciated states of affairs are ascertained by comparison and subsumption of two types of propositions. The propositions of the first type are general; they are inductive generalizations of many detailed descriptive propositions concerning the existing states of affairs. The propositions of the second type are also general statements describing the postulated facts (covered by the accepted valuations). A comparison of the actual with the postulated yields either a compatibility or a discrepancy between the two. The consequence of a discrepancy between what is actual and what is postulated is a negative evaluation.

If a negative evaluation is passed not with reference to the existing state of affairs but to the predicted direction of development of what is, the ensuing activity will be of a preventive character. In this case, what is the fact is not appreciated from the point of view of what ought to be (or from the standpoint of the accepted valuations), as in the corrective procedure. Here it is two non-existent states of affairs which are compared: what eventually will happen with what ought to; and it is only on this ground that what actually is becomes the subject of evaluation. For example, a frequent participation in swimming races by a person with a not very robust heart is negatively appreciated by a doctor, not because it causes illness at the moment but because it may do so in a more or less remote future. Thus, in this case a negative judgment of what is the effect now is a result of the finding of a discrepancy between what may eventually happen and what is postulated. It can be remarked, moreover, that if in such a case a positive overall evaluation concerning the prognosis of change is attached to the negative evaluation of the existing situation, then it becomes necessary to undertake a purposive action.

Generalizing the above considerations, it can be stated that a negative evaluation of the existing state of affairs is the first of the possible types of conclusions that can be entailed by the initial diagnosis, leading to either a corrective or a preventive action.

(2) When positively evaluated states of affairs are found to be lacking, or when some negatively evaluated ones not resulting from a former action are found to be present, the necessity for undertaking project-making activity can arise. By projecting we denote the particular type of purposive action which has as its aim the creation of a state of affairs that does not now exist.

How does the undertaking of a projective activity come about? Before it begins, propositions recorded in the phase of description are taken into consideration on the one hand, and descriptive propositions concerning the postulated state of affairs on the other. From a juxtaposition of these two types of propositions follows a statement concerning the existence or non-existence of what has been positively appreciated in the postulates. If it turns out that all or some of the postulated states of affairs are lacking, then it follows that what is lacking is the subject of evaluation. Also any appearance of negative states of affairs which happen to arise in the course of earlier activities in place of the intended ones can be ascertained. Such a situation can lead to undertaking purposive action aiming at elimination of the discovered deficiencies. For example, a system of education brings about results which in the main are consistent with its postulated aims, but the description of the results also discloses that the system fails to encourage talents for the plastic arts. Now, if we consider encouraging plastic talents to be an important aim of education, a relevant projecting procedure can be undertaken on the ground of the finding. In consequence, the subsequent purposive action will encompass attempting to attain, besides the results obtained up to now, the newly projected results as well.

Thus a negative evaluation of the existing state of affairs as a result of discovering that some positively evaluated effects are lacking is the second type of conclusion that can be entailed by the initial diagnosis, a conclusion leading to a projective procedure.

(3) The third type of possible conclusion is arrived at when an existing state of affairs is found to be consistent with one system of evaluations and at the same time inconsistent with another accepted system. Such a situation makes it necessary to postpone the purposive procedure until an overall judgment is pronounced, reconciling the two discordant appraisals. Thus, the finding that the evaluations of a given state of affairs are discrepant forbids purposive action before the overall judgment is pronounced, for the danger of such an action's being erroneous is considerable. The mode of reaching the pronouncement of final judgment aiming at establishment of the relationship between two (or more) systems of evaluation, or between competing sets of evaluative propositions within the same system of values, can be described as analytical-normative reasoning. Hence, if some state of affairs is evaluated in two or more incompatible ways, it will be necessary to carry out an analytical-normative reasoning process before any purposive action is undertaken.

The method of discovering this kind of discrepancy in evaluations can be briefly outlined as follows. What must be looked for are: (1) an agreement between descriptive propositions concerning an existing state of affairs and descriptive propositions based on evaluative propositions belonging to a given system of evaluations; (2) a discrepancy between descriptive propositions concerning an existing state of affairs and descriptive propositions based on evaluative propositions belonging to a different system of evaluations; (3) a discrepancy between descriptive propositions based on evaluative propositions of the given system of evaluations, and descriptive propositions based on a different system of evaluations. Discovery of any such discrepancies requires resolving which of the competing systems or which of the competing evaluative propositions should be considered as superior.

Thus, the third type of conclusion to be drawn from an initial diagnosis is a finding that analytical-normative reasoning is necessary in order to establish an ultimate judgment on the existing state of affairs and, in consequence, to decide whether some kind of purposive action is required or not.

It follows from the above considerations that the conclusion of the initial diagnosis is what determines the kind of purposive procedure that will be applied. The possibilities for purposive procedure are several. A conclusion negatively evaluating the given state of affairs points to the undertaking of a purposive procedure which is either corrective or preventive. A conclusion finding a positively appreciated state of affairs to be lacking points to the undertaking of a projective procedure. A conclusion showing an incompatibility of evaluations of the existing state of affairs points to some kind of purposive action after a prior analytical-normative reasoning. Sometimes, then, analytical-normative reasoning is a prerequisite for a projective, corrective, or preventive procedure. The analytical-normative reasoning effectuates arriving at the ultimate evaluation of the relevant facts.

Finally, it can be said that all purposive action depends on some negative evaluation of the existing situation. A corrective procedure stems from a negative evaluation of the *status quo* resulting from previous action; projective procedure stems from a finding of the *status quo* lacking positive evaluation, also a negative evaluation; preventive procedure stems from a negative evaluation of the direction of future events. If incompatible evaluations are involved, analytical-normative reasoning will reduce the case to one of the foregoing.

Various relationships between the types of purposive action are illustrated in Figure 3.

As can be seen from Figure 3, corrective procedure (seemingly the most frequent due to the essential inertia of human action in general) is called for on account of something that has been done earlier. Projective procedure is apparently twofold: it can take place either when some state of affairs is negatively appreciated, or when positive appreciation is lacking; in either case, it is a negative evaluation.

When we speak in general terms about purposive procedures (and

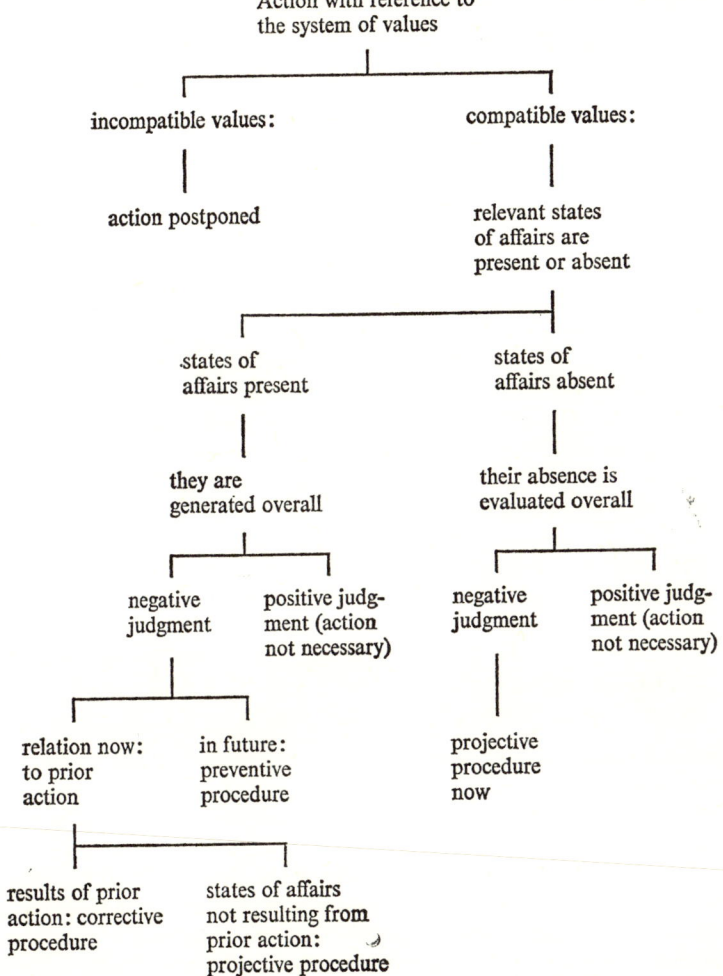

FIGURE 3

thus about all kinds of practical endeavors) we should not overlook a certain difficulty which is apt to appear when knowledge and action come together. Sometimes for an action to be effective it must be undertaken immediately. But decisions on what is effective action must be based on relevant knowledge, and this can only be supplied by researches which require time. The dilemma is between acting upon insufficient knowledge but with the chance that the results will be effective, or starting researches which might guarantee effective action, but perhaps too late.

Example

In 1948 . . . when Israel became an independent state, an organization in the United States which was concerned with the maintenance of civil rights for the Jewish population of this country was faced with strategic problems raised by the event for Jews living in the United States. The organization wished to base its decision about whether or not special action was called for on a scientific inquiry about the effect of the foundation of the new state on the United States population. Accordingly, a large-scale study was initiated based on a panel design. The analysis of the material proceeded for a prolonged period, in the course of which some very interesting results emerged together with important methodological advances concerning the use of panel designs. But in the meantime the world did not stand still. Israel largely disappeared from the headlines; public attention became more and more absorbed in other matters. The agency, actively engaged in its large-scale activities and consulted daily on many levels about problems of Jewish life, developed its strategy successfully without the benefit of the research. To be sure, the lasting value of the study will still bring credit to the agency which initiated it; its results may even in part find some application in future policy decisions. Yet from the point of view of its original purpose—which was to facilitate a decision on an acute problem of policy—the inquiry failed. The results came too late.[14]

Thus, the decision in the event of such a dilemma depends mainly on two judgments: on the appreciation of the risk of action without sufficient knowledge and on the appreciation of the urgency of action.

If we set aside this kind of difficulty, it can be said that the courses of projective, corrective and preventive procedures are essentially similar. After the initial diagnosis there is always the phase of formulating postulates and hypotheses, after which there is justification, project-making, control and judgment. Deviations from this general scheme can occur, due to the necessity to account for the known causal relationships, or to gain knowledge about some that are unknown, etc. As the projective procedure is less complex than the corrective—for it does not have to eliminate the effects of earlier activities—and also less complex than the preventive (though in this case eliminating effects of earlier activities is not involved), it is convenient to discuss it first. Following this, and a discussion of the problems of corrective and preventive procedures, I shall present the matter of normative-analytical reasoning, for there are elements in it which are absent from the three types of purposive procedure.

5 Elements of projective procedure

As has already been indicated, the course of the projective procedure begins with the initial diagnosis. After an initial diagnosis the conclusion of which shows a lack of positive appreciation of the existing state of affairs or negative appreciation of a situation not due to previous activities, and if a positive overall judgment is passed, then further phases of the diagnostic sequence are called for.

Postulating

By postulating I mean the description of a non-existent, imaginary state of affairs which is approved by evaluative propositions and is within the scope of the target for realization. In other words, the postulated state of affairs is the objective of the given activity. The concept of an objective is essential for any practical activity and the postulated state of affairs is of decisive significance for such activity in its several phases.

First, the postulated state of affairs, which describes positively appreciated facts, determines the range of facts to which an eventual practical activity will be directed. Second, the postulated state of affairs determines the forthcoming derived evaluations that will be recognized and accepted in the course of the practical activity. In the third place, the postulated state of affairs ought to be equivalent to the results brought about by the purposive procedure. Finally, the postulated state of affairs is the frame of reference for comparing the effects of an activity in order to find out whether that activity has been appropriate or not.

To establish what it is that is being aimed at, or what is designed to be the final consequence of a practical endeavor, is a necessary condition for summoning appropriate hypotheses[1] and for suggesting a reliable project. A faulty or insufficiently precise formulation of the postulated state of affairs can lead to working on the basis of hypotheses which, if realized, will bring about only a part of the postulated state of affairs, or results different from the postulated ones. For example, someone who wants to send a letter in some European countries by express air mail but fails to stick the 'express' stamp on the envelope will probably have his letter dispatched by regular mail in spite of the extra payment. Besides, if the postulated state of affairs is not precisely indicated, a faulty hypothesis is likely to be assumed. If a practical activity is to come to its end only on the attainment of the state of affairs identical with the postulated one, then a precise and sharp definition of what is postulated is necessary in order to be able to find out at all whether the given practical sequence can be considered as accomplished.

Lack of a precise indication of the postulated state of affairs can lead in consequence to the pursuit and attainment of something quite different than intended. If, for example, a woman orders a dress from her seamstress and fails to indicate the cut exactly, she risks getting a dress that will be quite different from what she had imagined (an authentic case settled in court). Thus a failure to define the objective of an activity properly is a consequential type of practical fallacy not at all infrequent in actual life.

Formulating hypotheses

If it is clear what the postulated effects are expected to be, a hypothesis ought to be formulated that will enable their realization. The formulation of a hypothesis concludes the diagnosis as an independent phase.

In connection with the formulation of hypotheses certain difficulties arise which seem to be peculiar to the practical sciences. Explanation, which is a reductive type of reasoning,[2] occurs when some effects are known and reasons or causes are sought for them. In the theoretical sciences it is principally the case that the effects are given as empirical, actually existing facts. The practical sciences are different from the theoretical ones in that, among other things, they seek to explain what is only postulated. Thus one of the peculiarities of the practical sciences is that they look for hypotheses to explain something that is not yet known, in terms of causes which have not yet been found to be efficacious (for at the time there is no way of checking them with reference to the effects). This peculiarity entails a risk that purposive action may eventuate in many practical fallacies. It can be objected that the theoretical sciences also attempt sometimes to explain what are not facts but potentialities. For example, the consequences of an increase in the discount rate for investments within a given economic system and at a given time can be theoretically considered. However, such considerations within theoretical discourse do not involve valuation.

The practical sciences make use of explanations of what is actually the case as well. This kind of explanation is particularly frequent in corrective procedures. In medicine, for instance, practical action is in principle corrective in character; it is very often necessary to find reasons for the existing and recognized data. In particular this is so when explanations are sought for negatively evaluated empirical data, viz. symptoms of some disease. However, even medicine, when it is engaged in preventive activities, deals with cases where explanations are sought for postulated, i.e. non-existent, facts.

When we speak of formulation of hypotheses, a reservation must be made that the methodology of the practical sciences does not undertake to deal with the psychology of creative effort, for it does not seem possible or correct to propose from the methodological standpoint any rules on how to be creative. No advice can be given, at least in purely methodological terms, for facilitating arrival at some valid hypothesis that remains to be discovered. The elements of invention evade our type of inquiry. At this point an element that is elusive of rational discourse—unaccountable, though indispensable—enters into science, practical as well as theoretical.

The problems of creative psychology seem to be situated on the borderline of many sciences and techniques. The methodology of the practical sciences is not directly interested in the psychological origin or determinations of any particular hypothesis. It is also not directly interested in the problem of the social determinations of the appearance of the concrete hypotheses, for this problem belongs to a theoretical discipline, namely to the sociology of science. However, it would be rash to declare that the methodology of the practical sciences is not interested in these problems at all. For it is easy to imagine a practical problem which consists not in discovering a hypothesis in order to use it for the solving of some practical task, but in which the discovery of a hypothesis is the practical problem itself, the task to be carried out. Then, all the advice concerning the practical procedures can be applied, while the problem itself is pushed one level deeper. For the methodological advice will then apply to the mental effort directed at seeking a basis for the hypothesis. In this purposive procedure, too, there will be an elusive element in the inception of the idea. However, the task can be facilitated by the methodology of the practical sciences, as it shows how by succeeding rectifications the effort can be concentrated on what is really important, i.e. on the discovery of an idea.

Justification

A diagnosis can be well or not so well justified. Thus, the formulation of a diagnosis is concluded by the setting forth of a more or less justified hypothesis or a set of hypotheses about what means ought to be applied in order to ensure the realization of the postulated state of affairs (viz. the objective of the given practical endeavor). Hypotheses cannot be set forth at will. They must be sufficiently justified.

By justifying a hypothesis in a projective procedure I mean, therefore, showing that it is probable that the given cause or set of causes is apt to bring about the postulated state of affairs.

In a projective procedure we can have simple or complex justification. It is simple if a definite relationship between two things is pointed out so as to provide the basis for realization of the objective (e.g., a tooth and its surrounding tissue can be anesthetized by means of the injection of an appropriate substance). A justification is complex when for the realization of the objective an aggregate of factual relationships must be resorted to. For example, suppressing adolescent aggression ('hooliganism') is possible only by creating and introducing various situations and motivations—ideological, social, economic, legal, etc.

Example

> One evening, the scout corps headquarters in one of the districts of Warsaw was entered by a very sullen-looking group. They looked around skeptically and one of them proposed in a voice which was not amicable at all: 'Well, you may send someone around to tell us what kind of bullshit that scouting of yours is.' The boys from the corps took the challenge and organized a sports team. Of course, it was not a normal team of boy scouts. Scouting in its usual version would not be feasible at all in such a setting. It was what some might call an unearthly team, but I would say it was right down to earth.[3]

The team served well the aim of resocialization. Justification of the projective procedure is explicated in the following passage:[4]

> A full resocialization of a boy or girl who has run wild requires the following conditions:
> First, the frustrating situations which cannot be resisted by a juvenile delinquent's frustration threshold must be eliminated from his or her life.
> Second, the threshold of frustration must be raised by training for emotional control based on suitable habits acquired in the course of carrying out definite tasks in life, such that these

become an expression of interests and plans for the future. What is involved is a life planning connected with a consequent motivation rooted in a set of consistent ideas and in some system for understanding and evaluating the world.

Third, adaptation must be cultivated, leading to elimination of attitudes which are effects of the past states of apathy, aggression and antisocial approach to the world.

Justification in the projective procedure can be based on established relationships between things (empirically grasped events) and only this type of knowledge can provide the frames within which the relevant factual relationships must be looked for. So, factual relations accessible in the existing knowledge, and in particular the causal relations, frequently allow basing the projective procedure on them. A projective procedure aimed at anesthetizing a tooth can be based, under normal conditions, on the familiar causal link between a temporary blocking of the nerves near and in the tooth and the absence of the feeling of pain in the treated area. However, a projective action is often urgently required even though some of the relevant factual relationships are inaccessible. In such a situation the need to discover them by means of appropriate research imposes itself. For example, the goal of suppressing adolescent aggression as a social nuisance imposes the need to explicate appropriate, hitherto unexamined social relationships so as to enable undertaking effective practical action.

It should be noted that needs of this kind, signaled by the practical sciences and often dictated by sheer necessity, stimulate a systematic increase of theoretical knowledge. Discoveries and inventions in the chemical industry made during the war, when the lack of basic raw materials and other means compelled scientists to seek for novel solutions, are well known.

Example (from the field of economy)

The director of the War Finance Division during the last war used research results very effectively to press for action. One illustration will serve to show how he did this. He knew, for example, from his experience as Chairman of the X State War Bond Committee, that personal solicitation was essential if substantial sales of bonds were to be made to large numbers of individuals. He discovered, also, after he became Director of the War Finance Division, that the chairmen of many other states did not accept *his* experience as a guide to what *they* ought to do. They shuddered at the thought of having to recruit and train tens of thousands of volunteers to serve as solicitors in war bond campaigns. Consequently, when he urged them to use solicitation and cited his own experience, they would solemnly

ELEMENTS OF PROJECTIVE PROCEDURE

assure him that their state was different from X state and that personal solicitation was not necessary to sell bonds in their state. The result was an impasse and, at first, several states did not use personal solicitation.

A study of the effectiveness of the Second War Bond Drive provided the director with data such as that shown in Figure 4. He had a brief pamphlet prepared which showed these and related results. He distributed these pamphlets to all the state and county war bond committees. He also had these results presented in the regional meetings in which the plans for the Third War Bond Drive were dis-

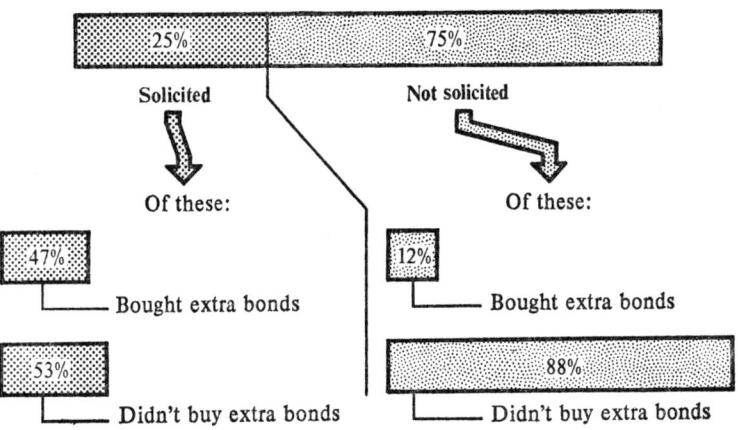

*Includes those whose wives were solicited

FIGURE 4

cussed and developed. The net effect of using the data in this way was that war bond committees convinced themselves of the value of solicitation. They recruited and trained a much larger group of solicitors. As a result, the number of people who were personally asked to buy war bonds increased from 25 per cent in the Second Drive to 50 per cent in the Third, and the sales of Series E Bonds almost doubled.

The impartiality of accurate measurements usually facilitates objective consideration of the facts, and this leads to the acceptance and implementation of effective policies. When decisions are made by pitting one person's experience and judgment against that of another, there is usually disagreement. Often the best decision is not made, and any decision that is made is accepted and followed only half-heartedly by many of the persons involved.[5]

As noted earlier, in the final phase of the diagnosis in a projective procedure a hypothesis or a set of hypotheses on how the objective ought to be realized is formulated. Of course, the formulation in itself by no means presupposes that the hypothesis properly apprehends the relationship between the factors described in it and the postulated objective.

Example. We can use the following considerations by R. K. Merton:[6]

> *Over-Specification of the Problem.* The policy-maker often assumes that he has precisely identified his particular problem and comes to the researcher with a specific request for research. But this may be premature specification. The researcher has the task of ascertaining the *central* pragmatic problem rather than passively accepting its initial specifications by the policy maker.
>
> 'Thus, a Jewish "defense agency" requests a research to determine which of alternative types of mass propaganda will probably be most effective in curbing anti-Semitism. This does not represent the *prime* objective which is "reduction of anti-Semitism." The policy-maker has prematurely included in his statement of the problem a specification of *means* as well as the end-in-view. The expert re-defines the practical problem. On the basis of previous researches, he indicates that deep-seated prejudices are not markedly vulnerable to propaganda campaigns. The problem becomes re-formulated: it is no longer an inquiry into efficiencies of alternative propaganda, but the comparative efficiency of a given propaganda campaign and of inter-religious voluntary organizations.'

The main aim of the justification phase is to determine the relationship of the hypothesis to the postulated state of affairs. In exceptional cases the justification can afford certainty. It can be made highly probable when it is based upon simple factual relationships, or upon well-established ones.

Because empirical phenomena are entangled in a network of interdependent relations, many such relations are at work in the course of the projective procedure while only some are recognized. It also frequently happens that while certain types of factual relationships are known on the general theoretical level, in an individual specific case their concrete pattern may be ambiguous; thus it is difficult to determine the degree of justification of the hypothesis. It seems reasonable to say that in the practical sciences no hypothesis can ever be considered as fully justified.

It is noteworthy that, contrary to the theoretical disciplines which pursue general knowledge in the first place, objectives of the practical disciplines often consist in realizations of certain narrowly defined individual states of affairs which are unique and unrepeatable. This is another reason why it is difficult to justify hypotheses in the projective procedure, for resort to general theoretical knowledge and to experimental knowledge in particular is limited and analogies, often misleading, have to be relied upon. The individualized tasks of the practical sciences do not facilitate reflection on or generalizing of their problems. This is perhaps one of the reasons for the relatively low level of theoretical awareness in these disciplines. However, it is still possible within the practical sciences for problems to be solved on a general level by discovering the patterns of realization of certain general types of tasks; in this way general knowledge can also be pursued by the practical disciplines.

In the course of a projective procedure, a hypothesis can be verified in either its initial or its final phase. An initial verification is one that takes place at the beginning of the process of justification; it is based on already available knowledge and does not require any new empirical material. A final verification is one that takes place after the realization of the project, and it is based on an analysis of the effects of its realization. Only the initial verification can be involved when we are discussing the justification of hypotheses in projective procedures.

The research procedure proper for the phase of initial verification was applied by Thorsten Sellin in his research concerning the model of a penal code. It is obvious that the death penalty is a problem which can hardly be investigated by arranging experiments and studying their effectiveness. Thus the validity of the proposition that the application of the death penalty leads to a decrease in capital crimes committed must be based on whatever available material there is. In trying to solve this problem, Sellin formulated a number of hypotheses which he verified in his work with reference to the existing empirical materials.[7]

It seems reasonable to assume that if the death penalty exercises a deterrent or preventive effect on prospective murderers, the following propositions would be true:
(a) Murders should be less frequent in states that have the death penalty than in those that have abolished it, other factors being equal. Comparisons of this nature must be made among states that are as alike as possible in all other respects— character of population, social and economic conditions, etc— in order not to introduce factors known to influence murder rates in a serious manner but present in only one of these states.

(b) Murders should increase when the death penalty is abolished and should decline when it is restored.

(c) The deterrent effect should be greatest and should therefore affect murder rates most powerfully in those communities where the crime occurred and its consequences are most strongly brought home to the population.

(d) Law enforcement officers would be safer from murderous attacks in states that have the death penalty than in those without it.

Initial verification of a hypothesis in the course of its justification runs along the following lines. When a number of hypotheses are available which might eventually prove to be relevant, an initial selection among the competing hypotheses ought to be made, or those hypotheses ought to be chosen which will be significant for the intended action. If, for example, we intend to make practical changes in a certain field of social relations—say, the trade unions—the first step would be a listing of the hypotheses attempting to describe and explain the social processes related to union activities. The next step would be to determine which of them are mutually competing, and which ones deal with separate aspects of the given field.

Example

We would suggest as a research hypothesis that the more centralized an industry, the more need for a union to be bureaucratic. . . . It may be stated as a general proposition, however, that the greater the bureaucratization of an organization, the less the potential within it for membership influence over policy formation. . . . More recent investigators have extended his analysis, pointing out that resistance to the authority of a new leader by the remaining staff of the old one leads him to institute allegiance to rationalized rules—that is, to increased bureaucratization. One might hypothesize on the basis of this analysis that when a trade union leader with charismatic attributes is succeeded without conflict, as in the case of Hillman, the union will become more bureaucratic. . . . The general proposition may be suggested, however, that the more diffuse the ideology of a trade union, the greater the likelihood of internal factionalism. . . .[8]

Bringing together the various data offered by available knowledge will result in weakening some hypotheses and reinforcing others.

Thus, the course of reasoning in justification as a part of the projective procedure runs from the postulated state of affairs treated as effects, to the causes underlying them. If it is believed that the given causes entail the postulated consequences, the hypothesis is tested.

The testing of a hypothesis consists in identifying the consequences known to be actually entailed in the causes included in the hypothesis and in checking to see if any entail consequences known to be false. If it turns out that the consequences entailed in the causes are all validated, the hypothesis can be accepted as testing positive. Moreover, if the validated consequences entailed in the causes include in their scope the postulated objectives, it can be taken for granted that the given causes hold for the postulated states of affairs.

Example. Let the postulated state of affairs be an increase in the efficiency of work of waiters (Z) and a system of payment proportional to the work done (S) be the cause. The hypothesis that efficiency of work is proportional to the payment received for it can be tested by looking for data in various occupational groups, social systems and periods of time, i.e. by looking for validating and invalidating consequences of the hypothesis. If it turns out that a system of payment dependent on individual output increases the efficiency, the hypothesis can be considered as justified. If, besides, the consequences entailed by the hypothesis have a broader scope (that which holds for the other occupations and jobs holds also for waiters), we can say that the given cause (S) also entails the postulated state (Z).

As the degree of justification of a hypothesis or a set of hypotheses depends on the available knowledge, the acceptance of hypotheses is frequently loaded with considerable risk. If the data on how they will work are deficient or scanty, the effects cannot be predicted with any great degree of certainty.

It may also be that immediate pragmatic process will serve to postpone theoretical analysis. Thus Merton has observed:[9]

> Not infrequently, applied research leads to an empirical finding which may be at once successfully applied, although the finding itself is not 'understood' (i.e. located) in theoretical terms. Thus, it may be found that provision for several rest periods in an industrial plant reduces labor-turnover, raises employee morale, etc. The plant manager who finds that his program 'works' may see no occasion for further research. If the research worker is not theoretically sensitized, he, too, may be content with this 'successful' application of an empirical finding. The fact remains that he has not yet identified the critical variable in this result: was it that rest-periods reduced fatigue? Or was it, possibly, that the degree of managerial concern with employees' problems (as symbolized by the rest-pauses) was the decisive variable? Or, again, was it the part played by employee representatives in arriving at the decision regarding rest-periods—in short, the manner in which this policy was introduced—that proved

basic? Unless the crucial theoretical variable in the concrete practice of rest-periods can be identified, there is no basis for assuming that the same results will be obtained on other occasions.

In this connection an objection can be raised. It may be said that in the course of the process of justification an attempt was made to find out by some simple and limited experiment, offering new empirical data, whether the given hypothesis actually facilitated the realization of the postulated objective. Such an attempt, remaining within the limits of justification of the hypothesis, would reinforce the probability of the proper choice. A successful experiment would result in developing the project, while an abortive one would lead to discarding the projective procedure in favor of a further determining experiment.

This might raise some doubts. A supposition that an experimental testing of a hypothesis belongs to its justification would blur the distinction between the chronological and the methodological sequence of the procedure. Though it sometimes happens that hypotheses are tentatively tested experimentally on a limited scale, we are apt to forget that experimenting is itself a purposive procedure and as such it requires a project, its realization and an investigation of the effects that have been brought about. Thus, minor tentative experiments are closed, independent units of purposive procedures are undertaken for the sake of the main purposive sequences.

There are reasons for selecting the initial verification as a separate phase of the purposive process. But in social policy, and in legal policy in particular, experimenting can only rarely be used as a research method, for the principle of equity forbids applying legal regulations to some persons and not to others. If, then, the experimental method can rarely be applied in legal policy, it is necessary to make an exact and efficient use of the data which are available without experimenting. This is the aim of the initial verification.

Independent of these general principles for the justification of hypotheses, detailed considerations of the problem for each particular field of practical science must be carried out. Here the difference between the social and the natural sciences should be emphasized again, for they differ as to the contents of hypotheses proposed in each of them. In the practical social sciences, where the number and ambiguity of evaluations are much greater than in the natural sciences and where the competing hypotheses are usually not sufficiently validated, various negative consequences of the merging of evaluative and descriptive propositions come to the forefront. These negative consequences appear most clearly when it comes to application of the political disciplines.

R. K. Merton describes various kinds of frustration which are brought about by this situation.[10]

These frustrations can be classified into two main groups: (1) those deriving from conflict of values between the intellectual and the policy-maker, and (2) from the bureaucratic type of organization itself.

1. Conflicts of values between intellectual and policy-makers:
(a) Occasionally the bureaucratic intellectual finds himself the target for conflict arising from different universes of discourse of the policy-maker and himself. Research which appears trivial from an immediately practical standpoint may be highly significant for its theoretic implications and may later illumine a series of practical problems. The intellectual is in time compelled to accept new criteria of significance.

(b) Research findings may be exploited for purposes which run counter to the values of the intellectual; his recommendations for policy based on the 'weight of the evidence' may be ignored and a counter-policy introduced.

(c) The intellectual will often not be willing to commit himself on the basis of what seems to him 'flimsy evidence,' whereas the policy-maker must do so because of the urgency for action.

(d) Specialists may experience frustrations from being required to work in fields which are outside their sphere of competence, since policy-makers are at times not clear on significant differences between specialists.

2. Frustrations arising from bureaucratic organization:
(a) Since bureaucracies are organized for action, questions are often asked of intellectuals for which they have no immediate answer. Or, this may invite the 'deadline neurosis': problems may be raised which it is impossible to solve within the allotted time.

The problem of the 'deadline' has perhaps been best described by Robert Louis Stevenson in an entirely different context:

'This is no cabinet science, in which things are tested to a scruple; we theorize with a pistol to our head; we are confronted with a new set of conditions on which we have not only to pass judgment, but to take action, before the hour is at an end.'

(b) Lines of communication between policy-makers and intellectuals may be clogged, leading typically to frustrations.

(1) Since policy-makers often do not keep intellectuals informed of impending problems of policy, it is difficult for the latter to determine what are relevant data.

(2) Or, there may be the problem of having research findings reach the appropriate policy-maker, who is confronted with a mass of material emanating from different sources.

(3) Or, the findings on their way to the policy-maker may be emasculated and distorted by intervening personnel.

(4) Or, finally, there is the problem of so formulating the findings that the most significant results will be intelligible to and engage the interest of the policy-maker. The 'processing of the material' may require simplification to the point where some of the more complex though significant findings are discarded.

(c) Despite all precautions, the intellectual's findings may not be used by those for whom it is intended. This eliminates the very rationale of the intellectual's work and dissipates his interest in his work, leading to the 'boondoggling neurosis.' (Correlatively, even occasional use of research findings, no matter how limited the context in which these have been put to use, will serve to reinvigorate the morale of the intellectual.)

(1) The policy-maker will at times reject funded research in the social sciences on the assumption that his first-hand experience has given him a more secure understanding of the situation than the intellectual can possibly attain. This is the more likely to occur if the findings suggest changes in familiar routines and practices, since it is seldom that the intellectual can demonstrate the greater effectiveness of proposed as compared with current arrangements.

Project making

Since there are on the one hand states of affairs to be realized, and on the other hypotheses informing how such realization might be feasible, for the realization actually to occur the postulated states of affairs must be projected or designed.[11]

The term 'project' can have at least two meanings. According to the first, we define project as '. . . a description of the projected action, work or product.'[12] The project in this sense, together with the decision for its realization, is equivalent to what has been termed within the diagnosis as the postulated state of affairs (the objective of practical activity). However, with the project so conceived, which is an indispensable and essential element of the initial diagnosis, an important qualification must be kept in mind. An example may help to clarify why the project as a description of an action and/or its product fails to encompass the project-making phase of the purposive procedure. A schematic design of some device, e.g. a tape recorder, is a description of the product, but it does not supply information on how it has been manufactured. The history of the chemical industry shows that while products have been stolen and subjected to minute scrutiny and analysis and then described exactly, and even their ingredients discovered, they could not be synthesized without access to the know-how of their manufacturing technology (presumably this is the case with the kind of paper on which the US banknotes are printed).

According to the second meaning, a 'project' is the purposive effort of one who 'attempts to devise the mode of performance of an action, work, or product.'[13] It is this meaning of the term which encompasses the requirements referred to in the above examples, since it specifies the necessary condition for the transition from hypothesis justification to realization of the objective of the purposive procedure. A project is the intermediate link in the transition. In this sense, it can be defined as a description of the arrangement of things in space and time in the course of their change.

The latter conception of project seems to fit better to the methodological requirements of the practical sciences not only for the reason given above but also because it seems to be in accord with common intuition. The former meaning, however, also seems to have some utility as a synthetic definition. In talking about objectives we often use ambiguous and unclear terms, so that it may be difficult to identify the scope of the given objective or of the set of objectives. As objectives are approved states of affairs, both such states and their evaluations appear as important elements. Most commonly, emphasis is laid upon evaluations, to the neglect of the descriptive aspect. This fact increases the chances for discrepant interpretations and for misunderstandings. It could be made easier to identify objectives if more attention were paid to description. Thus any social or legal policy in setting forth the aims it pursues ought to make sure at the outset that those aims have been expressed in empirical terms, so as to permit finding suitable means for their realization. If they have not been so expressed, an attempt should be made to translate them into empirical language. If such an attempt fails, it can be surmised that underlying the aims formulated in general and emotional terms there are some other objectives which can be identified on ideological grounds. If, on the other hand, the attempt is successful, it must be investigated whether the aims as formulated in empirical terms infringe on any socially accepted values.

Example. R. Pound lists the following aims and tasks of law, which he calls 'social interests':[14]

1. Common security achieved by legal norms guaranteeing security and social order and the protection of property and contracts;

2. Protection of such institutions of society as the family, religion, and the civil rights of citizens;
3. Protection of the moral sentiments of society;
4. Maintenance of social goods, expressed in laws protecting the goods indispensable for human life;
5. Guarantees of general progress, expressed in the support offered by law to economic, political, and cultural progress;
6. Protection of the life of the individual.

This list of aims, formulated in general and non-empirical terms but based on accepted values, offers no basis for an empirical description of any workable project, or of any workable social or legal policy which could be brought to life.

A project can be formulated in different languages, but its essential feature seems to be that it is formulated in verbal language. In that language, projects are formulated as purposive propositions. Thus, the proposition: 'In order to limit the number of economic offenses, the standard of living of the population must be increased and social control must be improved,' is a hypothesis translated into the language of a project. Projects can be expressed in legal terms as norms. Legal norms do not inform as to the aims for which they constitute the means, but they impose obligations and bestow rights, thereby contributing to the realization of the relevant objectives. From this point of view, norms are projects for behavior. In other words, legal regulations are projects of postulated states of affairs, briefly expressed as norms. Projects can also be graphically presented. But in all cases, purposive propositions are their basic form.

Realization of a project always requires some costs. As noted earlier, the decision that a project should be realized and not abandoned is the outcome of a negative evaluation of the existing state of affairs and a positive evaluation of the costs of realization, i.e. a positive overall judgment. Determination of the costs of a project consists in a comparison of the costs of realization of the project itself with the expected advantages of the results which will have been attained. Quite frequently special researches are needed to make this calculation.

Example. In the spring of 1959, social and cultural activists collaborating with the Regional Club of Ziemia Sądecka proposed initiating the publication of a regional periodical for Southern Poland. In order to gain some knowledge of whether there was any social demand for such a periodical, the management of RSW Prasa (the largest press-owner and publisher in the country) and the Regional Committee of PZPR (the Communist Party in Poland) in Cracow commissioned the Cracow Press Research Center to conduct a study to find out if a new periodical of this kind was demanded.

On September 23 and 24, 1959, 210,000 copies of a questionnaire were distributed in five districts of the region. Answers began to come in on September 25, and the last was received January 12, 1960. A total of 6,769 questionnaires, or 5·5 per cent of the distributed number, were returned.[15]

Project realization

To provide workable guidelines for action, the practical disciplines make use of directives some of which are scientific and some not. The directives of these disciplines which are *not* scientific, are: (1) decisions based on value judgments; (2) endeavors related to the constructing of hypotheses; (3) practical activities performed according to scientific principles (e.g. physical manipulations in experimenting).

The practical procedure differs from the theoretical as to the first point, though not altogether. In the practical disciplines value decisions are taken to change or not to change a particular situation, whereas in the theoretical disciplines utilitarian value judgments are made to continue or not continue examination of a given set of facts. The distinction bears importantly on the problem of project realization; as merely a task to be performed, project realization is a problem of skillful handling and thus not subject to methodological considerations. This is simply another non-scientific aspect of the directives of the practical disciplines. The second matter, relating to hypotheses formulation, is a psychological question and thus no objective guidelines for controlling the process of scientific creative effort can be given. The third, referring to the actual physical activities required by the project, does use relevant scientific techniques and implements, of course. But the physical activities themselves, though necessary to pass to the next phase of the projective procedure—the testing—belong to a different order of phenomena, to objects and behaviors.

The testing

After a project has been realized, the state of affairs that has been brought about should be tested. Testing, in the context of the projective procedure, means to find out whether the projected and the realized states of affairs are compatible. This is necessary in the case of the purposive procedure for, as noted earlier, the accepted hypothesis (or set of hypotheses) often has only a small or not easily definable probability. However, irrespective of the degree of probability of the hypothesis, the testing is necessary because a practical error might have been made in the course of the purposive procedure, leading to a result different from the one intended. A comparison of the postulated and realized states of affairs would thus reveal whether the hypothesis had been wrong or a practical error committed, causing a discrepancy between the expected and the actual state of affairs. If the postulated and realized states of affairs are in agreement, the purposive procedure has of course been correct.

The testing also makes it possible to describe the various kinds of results brought about by the purposive procedure. With reference to the matter of results and testing the correctness of the purposive procedure, a number of concepts must be introduced. These concepts are important for various kinds of purposive procedures, and in particular for the corrective procedure.

By results of a purposive procedure are meant its observable effects. By adequate results we shall mean results that are coextensive with the postulated state of affairs. To bring about an acceptable result is the sufficient condition for realization of the objectives of a purposive procedure. By inadequate results we shall mean those that are not coextensive with the postulated state of affairs. Intended results refer to those foreseen and accepted by the purposive procedure, while unintended results are unforeseen ones, both positive and negative.

Though it may seem paradoxical, there are both positive and negative results among the intended ones.[16] For example, certain negative effects are foreseen as the result of deciding to extract a tooth. But though the pain in the jaw after the extraction is a negative effect, it is an intended one because it is necessary in order to attain the positive result, i.e. the elimination of the aching tooth. Some losses simply have to be expected. Thus we have what can be termed the derivative or secondary effects encountered in the course of the purposive procedure; they are not expressly welcomed, but are ultimately accepted. The intended positive effects are of course those which have been postulated and are in no respect negatively evaluated.

As an example of unintended positive results we can think of someone who wanted to dig a well—this was his objective. He unearthed a bag full of gold, buried right at the spot of the well. Or more realistically, consider an experience from the Second World War in the Pacific area. American soldiers, not adjusted to the climate, very frequently suffered from malaria. A medicine called 'Avalene' turned out to be a very good remedy. It also turned out that some of those treated with Avalene against malaria suffered as well from arthritis and that the medicine was effective against that disease, too. Some of the malaria patients were thus cured of their arthritis. Such results are commonly called surplus gains.

The most undesirable results in a purposive procedure are unintended negative ones, for they can cancel the whole meaning of the procedure. In a volume of stories, *Sezam* by S. Lem, a fictitious case is described in which a computer helps to devise a chemical formula for an effective medicine against cancer. The medicine is synthesized and clinical tests confirm its superb efficiency. Cancer is completely eliminated, but its elimination is due to the fact that another and much more noxious kind of killer growth has been implanted. This may serve as an illustration of a purposive procedure in which the intended positive results are attained, but at the same time unintended negative results are brought about which are much worse than what has been eliminated.

From the above it can be seen that the most advantageous situation possible for a purposive procedure is when the intended effects can be fully controlled, and there are no derivative side effects. By the same token, the most undesirable situation is when secondary and unintended negative effects set in, without positive ones to offset them.

Evaluation of results

If we define the various types of results that can be the consequences of purposive procedures, we can evaluate these procedures. In evaluating the results of a purposive procedure from the standpoint of the accepted values, two problems must be considered. We have to assess the intended effects *and* the unintended ones. The following possible combinations of *factors present* can be listed:

1 All the intended effects; no unintended effects.
2 Some of the intended and no unintended effects.
3 All the intended and some unintended but positively appreciated effects; no unintended and negatively appreciated ones.
4 Only some of the intended and some unintended but positively appreciated ones; no unintended negatively appreciated effects.
5 All the intended and some negatively appreciated unintended effects; no positively appreciated unintended ones.
6 Only some of the intended effects and some negatively appreciated unintended effects; no positively appreciated unintended ones.
7 None of the intended effects and some positively appreciated unintended ones; no unintended negative effects.
8 None of the intended effects and some negatively appreciated unintended; no positive unintended.
9 All of the intended and some unintended, both positively and negatively appreciated.

10 Some of the intended, and some negative unintended, some positive unintended.
11 None of the intended; some unintended positive and some unintended negative.
12 None of the intended and no unintended effects.[17]

These logical possibilities are represented in Table 4:

TABLE 4 *Table of effects*

No.	intended	unintended positive	negative
1	+	−	−
2	±	−	−
3	+	±	−
4	±	±	−
5	+	−	±
6	±	−	±
7	−	±	−
8	−	−	±
9	±	±	±
10	±	±	±
11	−	±	±
12	−	−	−

+ = all effects present
± = some effects present
− = no effects present

Evaluation of the results of a purposive procedure can be based not only on judgments accepted in the phase of the initial diagnosis. It can also be based on supplementary judgments it might be necessary to make in subsequent phases of the procedure. For the evaluations accepted during the initial diagnosis can be either sufficient or insufficient to judge the effects of a given purposive procedure. However, the need to expand the catalog of value judgments does not necessarily testify to the fallacy of the purposive procedure. Frequently the proper set of evaluations can only be arrived at after several partial experiments which permit enlarging their scope. This principle of gradual interpolations holds also for hypotheses, which can well be modified in the course of the procedure. A wider concept of the course of purposive procedure is here employed, covering those cases in which the main procedure is interrupted by another one (an 'inserted' purposive procedure) to correct the course of the former.

When it comes to overall evaluations, cases 1 and 3 from the above list of 12 must of course be unconditionally positively appreciated, while cases 8 and 12 must be unconditionally negatively apprehended. The problem remains open as to what overall evaluations ought to be assigned to the other cases. It is quite clear that when the effects of purposive procedures are both positive and negative, an analytic-normative reasoning process is necessary to arrive at an overall evaluation.

All remaining cases (except numbers 1, 3, 8 and 12) require decisions as to whether corrective procedures should or should not be undertaken. The overall evaluation—negative or positive—depends on the prognosis for realization of the required change. It is necessary to decide what are the limits of tolerance for the failure of the intended effects to appear, and what are the limits of tolerance for the appearance of the negatively appreciated unexpected effects, provided that other unexpected but positive effects have appeared and if the intended results have been brought about.

In the ideal case evaluations of the results of purposive procedures and evaluations of their course should be kept distinct. An evaluation of the course of a purposive procedure, of whether to bring it to an end or continue on, depends on the prior evaluation of its results. In consequence, an evaluation of the results of a given purposive procedure entails, after a proper normative analysis, an evaluation of its whole course.

A proper estimation of the results achieved—both intended and unintended—is crucial to the practical activity, for it may sometimes be better to suffer the existing evil than to risk a costly procedure of further change and the possible setting up of eventual negative effects associated with the intended ones.

Example. Censorship is sometimes considered to be an efficient means for suppressing socially noxious publications. What is the overall evaluation of the effectiveness of censorship in the American experience?[18]

> Lillian Smith's *Strange Fruit* was adjudged obscene in Massachusetts in 1945, though it did not make a similar impression in other jurisdictions. Ernest Hemingway's *To Have and Have Not* was removed from public sale and public library circulation in Detroit in 1938, but continued to sell at a brisk pace elsewhere. Erskine Caldwell's *God's Little Acre* was successfully defended in New York in 1933 against charges initiated by the Society for the Prevention of Vice; but thirteen years later it was found to be obscene in Denver, and in 1950 was accorded that same distinction in Massachusetts. As recently as 1905 the Brooklyn Public Library excluded from the Children's Room those notorious novels, *The Adventures of Tom Sawyer* and *The Adventures of Huckleberry Finn* (the latter of which had been

banned from the public library of Concord, Massachusetts, as 'trash and suitable only for the slums'). In 1954 the Illinois State Library system directed that Hans Christian Andersen's *Wonder Stories* should be stamped 'For adult readers only.'

The same author summarized the situation as follows:[19]

In my estimation the proscription of writings because of their feared effects on accepted beliefs is not only unconstitutional but, on the most pragmatic basis, unwise. Since 1791 the First Amendment has stood as a safeguard of the freedom of expression. The doctrine of political freedom it is intended to implement is not a bit of eighteenth-century muddleheadedness. It reflects, rather, the lesson learned from history that truth cannot be established by proclamation and that belief cannot be created by extirpating non-believers. It embodies the faith that whatever may be the short-run gains or losses along the way, in the end the national safety is endangered far less by political freedom than it is by political suppression.

6 The corrective and preventive procedures

From the purely theoretical standpoint there is no difference between the projective and corrective procedures. For it is impossible to create something absolutely novel and it is also impossible to put existing things together so as to have a new entity completely unrelated to its constituents. If, then, any new realization of a project is a transformation of what exists, it is impossible to devise something completely unrelated to what has been there. Thus there is no essential difference between projecting and correcting—in both cases the existing pattern of things is changed. It can be said that all project making is a correction of or improvement on that which exists, while all corrective action is project making toward change of the existing state of affairs. The image is similar if we look at the projective and corrective procedures from the point of view of the objectives of the practical action. For both procedures aim at realization of the projected state of affairs, i.e. both pursue the objectives of practical action.

Thus, theoretically, the distinction between projective and corrective procedures is a matter of convention. However, such a convention seems to be meaningful. It permits distinguishing between two methodologically different courses of procedure. In the projective procedure, the existing state of affairs is negatively evaluated by pointing to the lack of certain desirable features, and the postulated features or desiderata are projected. In the corrective procedure, the presence of certain negatively evaluated states of affairs is at issue, these having to do with some earlier projective, corrective or preventive action, and a certain state of affairs is postulated as a modification of the earlier results. Thus the corrective procedure is undertaken when the fruits of some earlier action have become negatively appreciated and are ripe for change or repair. A corrective procedure as here construed cannot correct what has not previously been an object of practical handling, for it can be applied only to the results of a change previously brought about by such handling or action. What has never before been such an object can only be changed by projective or preventive procedures. For example, building a footbridge over a stream is a projective activity, while repairing it after a flood is a corrective one. To build a stone bridge in the place of a plank footbridge is corrective, while to build a dam would be preventive.

Not only material objects but also opinions and attitudes of people can be corrected or reshaped. The causal relationships which are then employed can work in some situations and fail to work in others.

Example

Shils and Janovitz studied the reasons for the small influence of Allied propaganda upon the Wehrmacht soldiers during World War II. They perceived these reasons to be the links between small informal groups (friends, family) and the broader formal structure of the army. A soldier could find more than official relationships within the army. His detachment or platoon became a group of friends. In families, among groups of friends, and in the army the same beliefs were shared. In such conditions, to accept the views presented in pamphlets and broadcasts by the Allies would cause conflict not only between a soldier and the army but also between him and his family and closest friends. The propaganda of the Allies came to be more effective when the basic camaraderie in the army began to disintegrate, among other things as a result of conflicts between solidarity with the family and with the army.[1]

The above considerations can be generalized by saying that there is no difference between the projective and corrective procedures except from the standpoint of the structure of the purposive procedure. If the agent has not acted on this matter previously, then by changing the existing state of affairs he undertakes a projective action; if he is changing the product of some previous action, his activity is a corrective one. What is important is not the identity of the agent, but the structure of the purposive procedure. For example, cement plants in California face the following problem. They have enough raw material, but the rising price of gas is increasing the costs of production. The main task is to use the gas as efficiently as possible. Here the problem of the so called 'second air' arises. Gas that heats the raw material also heats the surrounding air which escapes, causing a waste of heat. The problem can be reduced to finding a way to capture this thermal air for heating the raw material. From the standpoint of the whole process of cement production, the attempt to transform the negative effects (loss of heat) into positive ones (heating of the raw material) is a corrective procedure. But from the standpoint of the technology of heating, the procedure consisting in the use of the 'second air' is something novel, hitherto unknown, and thus it is a projective procedure.

The preventive procedure

The preventive procedure must be distinguished as a special class, though it is quite similar to the corrective. By preventive procedure we shall mean an action aiming to prevent some negative state of affairs that could appear in the future. It might seem that a preventive procedure can only be initiated when there is no negative overall evaluation of what presently exists, but such a view is not sound.

A preventive procedure may be indicated in two types of conditions: (1) a negative state of affairs is present in a germinal stage, or (2) it is not yet present at all but can reasonably be expected to appear.[2] Both the germinal negative state of affairs and the possibility of its appearance are negatively evaluated. A germinal negative situation inherent in a positive state of affairs can lead to a negative conclusion in the initial diagnosis. For it can happen that some germinal negative states of affairs develop dynamically and are apt to soon change the actual pattern and its evaluation. It can also happen that even when no negative state of affairs is actually present, the chances are high that one may arise; such a situation must be negatively evaluated. Thus we should not construe too narrowly the principle that for a purposive action to be started the existing state of affairs must be negatively appreciated. For a situation can be so appreciated even if all is going well for the time being but it can be reasonably predicted that untoward events will occur unless preventive action is taken.

Example. Someone bought a used but quite good car in Canada. He went for a trip with some friends and the car performed well. However, just before the end of the trip there was a noise and smoke in the engine and it suddenly 'burnt out.' As it turned out, Canadian cars require a change of oil about every 2,000 miles. Before the trip the car was in good order, but it was close to the critical limit of 2,000 miles since it had last been lubricated. The limit was passed during the trip and the negative outcome—the 'burning out' of the engine—came about. The fault of the members of the party was that while they appreciated the car as good, they failed to notice that it was necessary to change the oil. Because of their lack of information as to the car's performance requirements, no preventive measure was applied of putting the car in a garage for lubrication, though actually it could be reasonably predicted that negative effects would appear at some moment if preventive measures were not taken.

It can be said that the quantitative proportion of preventive and corrective suggestions is a measure of the maturity of a practical discipline. More preventive and few corrective actions mark a higher degree of maturity; the reverse proportionality is characteristic for less developed practical sciences. The introduction of automation in a technology bears witness to its high level of development, for one of the aims of automation is to prevent eventual negative processes. Preventive measures in medicine have such objectives as well. On the other hand, in legal policy a preponderance of corrective actions over projective procedures, and even more the preponderance of both the corrective and the projective over the preventive, is conspicuous. As a rule, a legislator initiates an action after things have gone wrong and only rarely because some negative state of affairs is foreseen.

It is not necessary to discuss the preventive procedure separately from the other types, for it differs from them essentially in one respect only. For a preventive procedure to be conceived and undertaken, something more is necessary than precise knowledge of the existing situation in the form of an exhaustive description of what presently exists. In a preventive procedure we need, besides knowledge of what exists now, an appreciation of what is likely to develop from it in the future. Thus, the preventive procedure requires knowledge of the regularities of development, an ability to foresee what will happen, for knowledge of the direction of development of what exists permits determining whether the present positively evaluated state of affairs is apt to be transformed into a new and negatively appreciated one. It can be said then that a preventive course of action requires not only static knowledge of what is, but also dynamic knowledge of what will be.[3]

Of course, to say this about the preventive procedure does not mean that knowledge of the regularities of development of the existing situation is superfluous for corrective and projective activities. Such knowledge can bring about significant and desirable modifications in projects or corrective reforms. It simply says that the lack of such knowledge makes preventive activities in general impossible.

Elements of the corrective procedure: diagnosis

The corrective procedure, like the projective and the preventive, consists of the following essential phases: diagnosis (description, evaluation, conclusion, postulating, formulation of hypotheses), justification, project making, project realization, testing, and evaluation of results. Though the corrective procedure does not differ from the other two types in its basic elements, still there are some characteristics which are peculiar to it. I shall attempt here to point out the differences between the corrective procedure and the projective.

To begin with, at the phase of the initial diagnosis the description refers only to those states of affairs which have been brought about, or have failed to be effectively changed, by a previous practical action. For while projective activity can be directed towards any state of affairs, a corrective procedure can deal only with what has been brought about by some previous activity.

The same rules that are applied when decisions are made to undertake a projective procedure hold when it is decided whether a corrective action is justified. It can be generally remarked that the conclusion of an initial diagnosis is a postulate to undertake a corrective action if it is ascertained that the negative effects of the existing state of affairs are worse than any negative effects that might be brought about by changing it. The undertaking of a corrective action is only justified if the overall diagnostic value judgment is positive.

In the further phases of the corrective procedure we can observe certain differences between it and the projective. Thus, at the phase of postulating the corrective procedure has a double purpose. On the one hand it deals with a state of affairs that has been brought about by a former practical action and is negatively perceived, while on the other it deals with a state of affairs that has been positively evaluated but failed to be realized. The postulatory phase of the corrective procedure therefore requires a description of the state of affairs that needs to be eliminated and of that which ought to be realized. This phase of the projective procedure is more narrowly conceived: it only attempts to describe the state of affairs that has been positively evaluated and is encompassed in the decision to realize it. While the projective procedure also deals with negative states of affairs, this is so only in regard to the absence of positively appreciated and not the presence of actually existing negative conditions.

In the last phase also of the diagnostic procedure, i.e. that of the formulating of hypotheses, certain differences between the projective and corrective procedures can be observed. At this stage the corrective procedure may have a twofold perspective. It can either pursue hypotheses aiming at elimination or neutralization of a negative state of affairs that has arisen, or it may be required to propose a hypothesis aiming at realization of a state of affairs that has been postulated earlier but failed to be realized. We deal with the first type when an earlier projective procedure has realized not only the postulated state of affairs but other, unanticipated, ones that are appreciated negatively. To take a fictional example, one of the characters in the novel *Exile* by Lion Feuchtwanger takes a sleeping pill in the evening, along with a pill to prevent headache in the morning as a side effect of the barbiturate. If he had taken the analgesic pill in the morning when he was actually suffering from the headache, it would have been a typical corrective procedure, acting on a hypothesis for getting rid of the negative effects of a previously intended and realized action. As it was, the taking of the two pills together is a combination of the projective (to induce sleep) and preventive (to prevent headache) procedures. The second type of case arises when the earlier projective procedure has realized its intended effects only to a limited extent and an unintended negatively appreciated state of affairs has been brought about, or if the previous projective procedure has brought about only negative effects.

To sum up the above, it can be said that the following occasions for the corrective procedure can be discerned:

(1) When all of the intended effects and some unintended negative effects are present,

(2) some of the intended effects are present and negative unintended effects are absent,

(3) some of the intended effects and some unintended negative effects are present,

(4) intended effects are lacking and unintended negative effects are present.

In cases (3) and (4) at least two hypotheses are required, one to bring about all the postulated effects and the other to get rid of the negative effects. In cases (1) and (2) at least one hypothesis is required, either to bring about the absent positive effects, or to get rid of the present negative ones.

These differences between the diagnostic phase of the corrective and the projective procedures account for the different sequences of justification in the two types of purposive action.

Justification

Initial justification of a given proposition with reference to the expected consequences is based, in the corrective and projective procedures alike, on available knowledge. However, in the corrective procedure the process of justification as a whole is more complex.

The most simple case is that in which all the postulated effects have been realized, and some negative ones have appeared. The task of justification is then to find out what it will take to eliminate the negatively appreciated effects. The search for such means proceeds by gradual elimination until what is left is believed, according to the best knowledge, to be the most efficient way of eliminating the negative phenomena or facts. A more complex case is that where, besides elimination of the negative effects, ways have to be found that will permit realizing the postulated state of affairs which has not been brought about. As noted above, such a situation requires at least two hypotheses.

However, this is not an exhaustive list of all possibilities. The descriptive part of the diagnosis in the corrective procedure must pay close attention to the fact that even though the cause or causes of certain negative effects are identified and eliminated negative effects may still remain, for it can well happen that additional negative effects will have been introduced. For example, if the operation of an engine has been impaired by insufficient lubrication, adding more oil can sometimes be an insufficient remedy. For besides the malfunctioning of the engine, the lack of oil may have caused other negative effects as well. The bearings may be damaged, thus working independently to produce new negative effects. In the diagnostic phase of the corrective procedure all the potential negative effects should be taken into account, so that the eventual chain of mutual relationships can be apprehended.

This points to a further difference between the projective and corrective procedures, as well as to a certain similarity between corrective and preventive actions. The main task of the diagnostic description in the projective procedure is to describe a state of affairs that does not yet exist, and which fact has been negatively appreciated. The task of the subsequent phases of project making is to discover the possible means of bringing about the postulated objectives. Any state of affairs incompatible with the accepted evaluations is then a negative state of affairs.

Things look different when we deal with diagnostic description in the corrective procedure. For in this case an actually existing state of affairs may be in itself, if taken separately, quite consistent with the accepted values, but may at the same time be the cause of another state of affairs which is negatively appreciated. For example, some type of ball bearing may be quite good but will work poorly in a given type of mechanical device. The diagnostic description would therefore consider the effects of the work of the bearing in that particular mechanism as faulty. A negative evaluation of this type of bearing can only be made in respect to its application to the given mechanism. In such a case, what is described is not only the negative consequences of the work of the bearing but also the construction of this particular device, which might be quite good with the use of some other bearing. Such a state of affairs must be part of the description because—and this is peculiar to the corrective procedure —once the negative effects are recognized the multiple elements related to them can be examined in order to determine why these effects have appeared in what had been intentionally arranged.

Thus in the corrective procedure more than in others the diagnostic description must contain knowledge of the relevant relationships, and of the causal ones in particular, for it is such knowledge that makes it possible to locate the causes of what has been found faulty.

In consequence, the formulating of hypotheses and their justification must cover the following types of cases:

(1) Justification of a hypothesis (or hypotheses) concerning the elimination of a negative state of affairs due to the effects of a previous activity.

(2) Justification of a hypothesis (or hypotheses) concerning the modification of a state of affairs which has been otherwise positively appreciated but which has brought about certain negative effects.

(3) Justification of a hypothesis (or hypotheses) concerning the realization of the postulated states of affairs which has failed to be realized in the course of earlier action.

The scope of choice of hypotheses is frequently limited by values accepted in advance. For a system of values can and should make provisions as to the means that can be legitimately applied. Such evaluations will probably eliminate or at least discourage some of the suggested manners of action.

Example

The emphasis on remedies carries with it one further emphasis. The one certain remedy for delay in any court system is the creation of a sufficient number of additional judgeships and it needs no special study to tell us that. But the question that deserves careful study its what can be done about court congestion apart from asking for additional judges. The creation of new judgeships raises complex political issues and is persuasive only as a last alternative. Only if there are no other avenues left for reducing delay is the case for additional judges compelling, since the maintenance of prompt justice for its citizens is a fundamental cost that society must bear. This study is primarily devoted to a systematic examination of remedies other than the ultimate one of additional judges.[4]

Project making, project realization, testing, evaluation of results

As in the other types of procedure, in the corrective procedure we can use various means of realization of the intended objectives. They can be means related to whole classes of objects, or they can be more individualized. Extreme examples of individualization of means are offered in such cases as when the personality of the agent is itself the means of action. This occurs most frequently in education, psychotherapy, etc.

Example

> In my practice as a therapist I have never had the experience of a dramatic revelation that immediately caused the patient to change. Usually it takes many hours of slow, careful work before changes, dramatic though they may be, begin to take place. Hollywood and some of the more sensational writers on the subject of psychoanalysis have made it seem a *tour de force*—producing a sudden break-through into health. Perhaps it is possible to do this. I haven't had that experience.[5]

The other phases of the corrective procedure do not reveal any essential differences from the course of the projective procedure. As in the latter procedure, once no negative and all the positive effects are found to be present, the corrective procedure should be considered completed. If the presence of some negatively appreciated effects or the absence of all or some of the positive intended effects is found, it should be determined whether it is reasonable to continue the corrective procedure.

As observed earlier, various types of purposive procedures can complement each other. We have already noted the complementary working of the preventive and projective procedures. Corrective and projective activities can also reinforce each other. For example, it may turn out that if it is impossible to eliminate the causes of certain negative effects, or if such elimination would bring about new adverse effects possibly even more negative than those eliminated, a projective procedure ought to be applied. For by projecting a certain state of affairs results may be obtained which while not eliminating the cause of the negatively evaluated state of affairs will eliminate or alleviate the effects. In the case of partial deafness the handicap may be overcome either by a surgical intervention which is dangerous and brings about negative side effects (a corrective procedure) or by applying a device for the amplification of sounds.

7 The analytic–normative reasoning process

It is frequently difficult to start a purposive procedure because the state of affairs which it is proposed to change is appreciated in different and incompatible ways. The same facts or situations can be differentially evaluated, and in consequence different overall evaluations can be entailed. For in some cases certain evaluations within the initial diagnosis conduce to undertaking a purposive procedure, while other evaluations conduce to renouncing action. What should be done then? Which of the incompatible evaluations should underpin the conclusion of the initial diagnosis?

As an example of this kind of discrepancy, we can cite the instance of major project proposals in two river valleys in the USA.[1]

> Proposals for public improvements on two rivers, like many legislative problems, have numerous 'angles.' The Kings River project was criticized by asking, 'Are efficient means being used to achieve a public benefit?' and 'Is the principle of equal opportunity being observed?' The Tennessee Valley Authority faced these criticisms, too, but the pragmatic effort of the TVA administrators to solve problems of conflicting interest made relevant two additional questions: 'Is the national welfare being subordinated to regional welfare?' and 'Is the regional welfare being identified with the interests of well-organized groups?'

It seems that some such difficulties, frequent as they are in practice, can be disposed of by a normative analysis preceding the purposive procedure. The difficulties can be resolved differently in different situations.

In the first place, three basic possibilities must be distinguished. The first is when a complete and non-contradictory system of evaluative propositions is available. The second is when an incomplete system of evaluations turns out after completion to be non-contradictory. The third is when there is a complete incompatible or contradictory system of evaluative propositions. Normative-evaluative reasoning can be applied in the first and second cases, but not in those where evaluative propositions are derived from complete and incompatible systems.

If there is a non-contradictory system of evaluative propositions available and a collision of norms occurs, directives determining the degree of validity of the relevant propositions have to be applied. On the ground of such directives, the evaluative propositions which hold for the state of affairs under consideration will be selected, and thus the overall evaluation, or the conclusion, will be established which is the valid one from the standpoint of the whole normative system.

Frequently, in order to determine the relevant directives, it is necessary to undertake research concerning the accepted values. There are many methods for empirical study of attitudes in general and of valuations in particular. One of these is simply to record relevant valuations that have been expressed. This method was used, for example, by R. K. White in a paper dealing, among other problems, with evaluative utterances contained in speeches by F. D. Roosevelt and Adolf Hitler before the Second World War. A simplified comparison of results in percentages can be presented as in Table 5:[2]

TABLE 5

	Hitler	Roosevelt
	%	%
Value of force	34·8	15·2
Ethical values	38·0	28·3
Economic values	10·8	27·7
Other values	16·4	28·4

Recourse to evaluations need not mean that they are sanctioned. Moreover, knowledge as to widely held values is gained not by collating declarations concerning those values but by examining the underlying emotional attitudes (acceptance or its lack) toward definite problems.

Example. L. P. Crespi suggests the following 'social rejection thermometer' to measure feelings toward conscientious objectors to the military draft:[3]

> The scale was constructed along the lines of the Bogardus Social Distance test and attempts to measure the degree of social rejection that one may feel toward individuals who are

CO's. The scale consists of a 'thermometer' running from complete neutrality or no rejection at zero degrees, to extreme rejection at 100 degrees. At every 20 degrees a statement appears describing the amount of rejection indicated by the position. While this scale is approximate, in that the steps have not been demonstrated to be equally spaced with precision, it was employed to provide some indication of the *action* an individual might take toward CO's, as contrasted to his more ideational position expressed by the graphic self-rating scale. The statements were roughly spaced by a quasi-Thurstone technique, giving empirical assurance that they were properly ordered, at least. The statements employed were as follows:

- 100° I feel that conscientious objectors should be shot as traitors.
- 90°
- 80° I feel that conscientious objectors should be imprisoned.
- 70°
- 60° I don't want anything to do with conscientious objectors.
- 50°
- 40° I would accept conscientious objectors only so far as having them for speaking acquaintances.
- 30°
- 20° I would accept conscientious objectors only so far as having them as friends.
- 10°
- 0° I would treat a conscientious objector no differently than I would any other person, even so far as having him become a close relative by marriage.

It may be observed that this thermometer differs from the graphic self-rating scale in that it does not allow for degrees of approval of CO's. Its most favorable position is neutrality. It differs also, as has already been mentioned, in that it presumably measures how an individual would behave toward CO's rather than how he feels toward them. Although these two reactions have much in common, an 'action' scale, the writer felt, might provide useful supplementary information.

By means of similar techniques certain emotional states can be studied (relevant data could be collected for further analysis and interpretations), shedding light upon more general attitudes and thus revealing approval or disapproval of certain value judgments.

Such a scale is used for experimental measuring of fear during combat:[4]

> Soldiers who have been under fire report different *physical reactions to the dangers of battle*. Some of these are given in the following list. How often have you had these reactions when you were under fire? Check one answer after each of the reactions listed to show how often you had the reaction. Please do it carefully.

There followed 10 items, each with a four-step check list. For example:

Shaking or trembling all over.
—— Often
—— Sometimes
—— Once
—— Never

A scale picture indicated that 9 of these items formed a very satisfactory scale when ordered as follows:
1. Urinating in pants
2. Losing control of the bowels
3. Vomiting
4. Feeling of weakness or feeling faint
5. Feeling of stiffness
6. Feeling sick at the stomach
7. Shaking or trembling all over
8. Sinking feeling at the stomach
9. Violent pounding of the heart.

In addition to such empirical investigations, it is necessary to know the formal directives determining the hierarchies of value judgments. In this way we may be able to gain insight into the scope and rank order of the recognized values and attitudes assumed by a person or a group of people, although it is not the intention to decide which values are proper and which are not. It should be noted that the directives determining the validity and rank order of values can be quite different in different value systems. There are directives to the effect that if there is a clash between a general and a particular proposition, it is the general proposition which must be held valid. But there are also directives holding that the particular proposition is predominant, e.g. the legal principle 'lex specialis derogat legi generali.' Finally, there are directives to the effect that norms of a certain kind are superior to certain other norms. For example, according to present Polish law, norms of a legislative bill are hierarchically superior to norms of an administrative order, which are in turn superior to norms enacted by decision of a particular management, etc. There is also a hierarchical pattern in ethics. If a child of a starving family steals something valuable from strangers in order to feed the family, that fact will be evaluated in terms of two norms which have clashed: 'Thou shalt not steal' and 'You must not allow your family to starve'; the final judgment will depend on which of the two norms is decided to be superior. Sometimes in the case of a clash of directives the directives of a higher order can be summoned. Thus, within a system of evaluative propositions, there are certain propositions which determine the rank order of preference among them. Judgments as to the weight of the particular norms are made in terms of such higher order directives. If no such commonly accepted directive as to the hierarchy of norms can be found by those judging, say, the above case of larceny, it can be said that the two norms in collision belong to two different and incompatible systems of norms. In such cases the analytic reasonings concerning evaluations take a different course and do not always lead to a final solution. For the same state of affairs is evaluated positively and negatively at the same time, in terms of two different kinds of value judgments (or two different sets of value judgments). It may then be particularly difficult to decide whether a purposive procedure should or should not be undertaken, for the different value judgments may point toward different and opposing solutions.

Two remedies can be suggested if a discrepancy between systems entailing evaluative propositions is discovered. The first would consist in determining whether the unreconciled normative systems have some norms which are compatible. If there are such compatible norms in the two systems, and if they are norms of higher order than those which are in collision, the validity of the latter is then determined in terms of the higher order compatible norms. Such a solution is based on the proposition that not all of the evaluative judgments belonging to incompatible value systems must be contradictory; there are compatible evaluations which belong to different and incompatible value systems. For example, a Catholic and an atheist both accept the norm 'Thou shalt not kill,' though their systems may be in some respects incompatible.

The second kind of remedy would be applicable when there are no compatible norms and directives in two systems that have clashed, and it might therefore be impossible to determine which of two contradictory norms ought to be held as valid in a given situation. In such a case, the eventual effects of a purposive procedure can be predicted and evaluated in terms of a third value system, accepted by both parties. The effects of each of the two systems can be evaluated, and priority given to the system which promises the more advantageous results, judged in terms of the third system acting as a kind of umpire.

Example. At a conference on family law, held on April 9–11, 1952 at Duke University, the following problem was considered: Is it preferable to give a Catholic child to a Jewish family who would guarantee it a good education but in a different faith, or to give it to a Catholic family which could not offer as good material conditions? A solution would not be difficult if a third system were accepted by both Catholic and Jewish partisans, pertaining to the welfare of the child construed in more general terms than religion (a properly educated child will be able to choose its religion when it grows up).

The essential question arises here as to what should be done if there are discrepant evaluations of a described state of affairs and no higher order norms to solve the conflict. We should note that the problem would be fallaciously conceived if we gave up in advance the effort to solve it, forgetting that though there might be no directives for the solution at the moment, nothing prevents us from seeking to establish them by way of reasoning. If this is done, the conflict may well be resolved in either of the two ways indicated above. But how can we resolve a real and not spurious contradiction of value judgments? The difficulties tend to pile up when there is no supreme value judgment to resort to, or when the subject initiating the purposive procedure is not an individual but a group or even an aggregate of groups. In such cases, the validity of certain evaluative propositions is as a rule determined by some procedural directives, accepted previously or coined *ad hoc*, offering the principles for reconciliation of value judgments. Such directives can describe procedures for balloting, for deciding or solving public affairs, recognizing authorities, defining the scope of free individual decision, relying on experts, etc. One example is the institution of arbitration. Two parties represent opposing systems or scales of values. Though neither is apt to respect the system of the other, both accept the general directive that it is better to abide by a solution offered by a neutral system (respected for one reason or another by both parties) than to leave the problem unresolved or seek to impose one's own solution by means which are believed by both to be illegitimate (e.g., by force).

In the case of incompatible whole systems it is possible that there is not only no agreement as to the evaluation of the matter at issue but also a lack of agreement as to the procedure for arriving at a solution. In such a situation it is of course not possible for the parties to determine objectively whether it is reasonable or not to undertake some purposive action. Withdrawing from a partnership, *votum separatum* of a judge, starting a war—these exemplify the not infrequent cases when it is impossible to arrive at evaluations that would be at least to some extent compatible. In such cases we encounter the difference between the institutions of arbitration and mediation. In arbitration, the evaluations are discrepant but there is an *a priori* agreement to accept the solution, even if it is incompatible with cherished systems of values. In mediation, the evaluations are in collision and there is no commonly accepted ground except the postulate that some rules ought to be sought for, though without any promise that they will be accepted when they are found. Thus there is no certainty that a solution will be arrived at, only the possibility that some still non-existent reconciliation will be found.

We have discussed so far only some of the problems related to the normative-analytic reasoning process. The process itself is of a complex character, and can perhaps best be described by means of a concrete example from the literature. The following is a series of evaluations reflecting 'a wealth of contradictory assumptions' inherent in the American model for societal behavior.[5]

1. The United States is the best and greatest nation on earth and will always remain so.

2. Individualism, 'the survival of the fittest,' is the law of nature and the secret of America's greatness; and restrictions on individual freedom are un-American and kill initiative.

But: No man should live for himself alone; for people ought to be loyal and stand together and work for common purposes.

3. The thing that distinguishes man from the beasts is the fact that he is rational and therefore man can be trusted, if let alone, to guide his conduct wisely.

But: Some people are brighter than others; and, as every practical politician and businessman knows, you can't afford simply to sit back and wait for people to make up their minds.

4. Democracy, as discovered and perfected by the American people, is the ultimate form of living together. All men are created free and equal, and the United States has made this fact a living reality.

But: You would never get anywhere, of course, if you constantly left things to popular vote. No business could be run that way, and of course no businessman would tolerate it.

5. Everyone should try to be successful.

But: The kind of person you are is more important than how successful you are.

6. The family is our basic institution and the sacred core of our national life.

But: Business is our most important institution, and, since national welfare depends upon it, other institutions must conform to its needs.

7. Religion and 'the finer things of life' are our ultimate values and the things all of us are really working for.

But: A man owes it to himself and to his family to make as much money as he can.

8. Life would not be tolerable if we did not believe in progress and know that things are getting better. We should, therefore, welcome new things.
But: The old, tried fundamentals are best; and it is a mistake for busybodies to try to change things too fast or to upset the fundamentals.

9. Hard work and thrift are signs of character and the way to get ahead.
But: No shrewd person tries to get ahead nowadays by just working hard, and nobody gets rich nowadays by pinching nickels. It is important to know the right people. If you want to make money, you have to look and act like money. Anyway, you only live once.

10. Honesty is the best policy.
But: Business is business, and a businessman would be a fool if he didn't cover his hand.

11. America is a land of unlimited opportunity, and people get pretty much what's coming to them here in this country.
But: Of course, not everybody can be boss, and factories can't give jobs if there aren't jobs to give.

12. Capital and labor are partners.
But: It is bad policy to pay higher wages than you have to. If people don't like to work for you for what you offer them, they can go elsewhere.

13. Education is a fine thing.
But: It is the practical men who get things done.

14. Science is a fine thing in its place and our future depends upon it.
But: Science has no right to interfere with such things as business and our other fundamental institutions. The thing to do is to *use* science, but not let it upset things.

15. Children are a blessing.
But: You should not have more children than you can afford.

16. Women are the finest of God's creatures.
But: Women aren't very practical and are usually inferior to men in reasoning power and general ability.

17. Patriotism and public service are fine things.
But: Of course, a man has to look out for himself.

18. The American judicial system insures justice to every man, rich or poor.
But: A man is a fool not to hire the best lawyer he can afford.

19. Poverty is deplorable and should be abolished.
But: There never has been enough to go around, and the Bible tells us that 'The poor you have always with you.'

20. No man deserves to have what he hasn't worked for. It demoralizes him to do so.
But: You can't let people starve.

How to solve antinomies of this type? The concept of global ethics might be helpful in resolving the perplexing problem of ethical contradictions. If so, what is the leading idea of this concept?

In order to introduce this concept a brief description of individualistic and socially oriented ethics is needed. In the present complicated and perplexing social world, composed mainly of agencies, institutions, organizations and bureaucracies, individuals tend to behave according to the old, almost endemic patterns of ethics which have been generated in small groups according to the norms which regulate face-to-face situations. New, more comprehensive ethics which grasp effects of social engagements and take into consideration supra-personal aims and goals emerge subsequently. These processes, which we observe in a state of being born, need more detailed empirical investigation.

By individually oriented ethics we mean a set of norms regulating the social behavior of people in which the predominating norms are those which regulate behavior towards other members of small, more or less informal, groups. Thus, in general, individualistic ethics condemn thieves, killers, adulterers, frauds, false witnesses; i.e. those who bring harm to others in 'face-to-face' relationships. Even if such behaviors do not actually occur in some narrow circle of people who know (or can know) each other, evaluations remain generalizations of experiences of this kind. Consequently, underlying the norms of individualistic ethics are various elementary types of behavior approved or condemned in narrow human contexts.

On the other hand, norms of socially oriented ethics refer to the social roles and positions which are or can be taken by an individual. The predominant aspect of such types of ethics is that they do not evaluate the personal qualities of an individual nor various elements of his conduct as a person, but rather the effects caused by the fact that he occupies a definite position in the social structure.

Ideological battles which are, almost everywhere, present in an open or a hidden way contribute to the increase and scope of the acceptance of instrumental attitudes: when authorities fight among themselves they mutually destroy the respect which they might possibly have had, without necessarily creating new types of higher values. Stable societies and subcultures, through the routinized processes of internalization, reinforce the tendency towards principled attitudes; societies, social groups or milieux undergoing rapid changes spread instrumental attitudes—indeed, these seem to be functional to finding a way of adaptation in a changing world. Ideologies survive when they are supported by principled attitudes. Their lives are in doubt, or might be placed under constant pressure, whereas as residuum they take on instrumental ones. Attitudes, as they are distributed among people, are not necessarily either wholly principled or wholly instrumental. Instrumental attitudes in the area of business might, to some extent, influence attitudes toward sex, but not necessarily so. Principled attitudes towards law and morality might have a tendency in certain circumstances to cover additionally different parts of personal life.

Traditionally people have a tendency to extend the norms of private life, and of private ethics, into the sphere of public life. But modern life shows quite shockingly that the old ethics, structured in this way, fail. Socially oriented ethics emerge as a relatively new device to cover and regulate those areas of human behavior which are primarily connected with the new, large, somewhat artificial entities in which the life of a modern citizen is submerged—institutions, organizations, agencies, factories, etc.

Some recently generated cultures (or subcultures; so called counter-culture is probably one of the possible expressions of them) which contain elements of socially oriented ethics might be immune to the disease of passive neutrality which is recently so visible in the face of injustices inflicted on various categories of individuals, groups and nations. On the other hand, such rationalization devices as dehumanization, deindividualization, depersonalization—in many societies—might easily be recognized as additional means designed to overcome the still dominating residue of individually oriented ethics. The erosion of ethics of this kind (and the trends of social change apparently go in this direction) would give a supportive incentive to commit administrative atrocities which now become the major source of dissatisfaction and possibly deviance. Additionally, the present underdevelopment (despite the tendency of growth) of the socially oriented ethics operates in a vacuum which might inspire the flourishing of different categories of violent ideologies. When the guidance of the traditional ethics is lacking, these ideologies, being without feeling on the interpersonal level, act as a palliative device in providing a general framework for behavior which is thus regarded as being regulated by ethical norms. So, then, a question arises: how might there be established norms which have features of general validity when individually oriented ethics do not fit to the complex world of institutions and organizations, when socially oriented ethics have only begun to emerge, and when abstract ideologies still do not grasp individual uniqueness and personal involvement in respect to social problems?

In order to try to find an answer to this basic question let me make a short semantic digression. Accepted social norms petrified into the code of the prevalent social system might be regarded as point zero. Deviation, then, is a (positive or negative) departure from this point. If so, then, apparently the question: What are the objective features of deviance? is at present unanswerable; the proper question should supposedly be formulated as follows: Who labels whom, according to what standards, as deviant? The answer is, then, also complicated. The individual might be labeled as deviant from the point of view of the group. But he might respond with the statement that the group as a whole is abnormal. In such case the more general norms of a subculture could be recalled as a standard measure. Still subcultures might be criminal, pathological, perverse, etc. To meet this, more basic norms of the social system could enter into the picture. But again: there exist social systems which might as a whole be regarded as deviant. If so, where does the escalation of the use of the metanorms lead? The answer is: to the ultimate values generated in the form of the various Weltanschauungen accepted by mankind. But, again, which values are final and ultimate when different Weltanschauungen offer and stress different virtues? The answer to this essential question is not given: it might and should emerge as a response to the accumulated problems.

Anyway, the picture which emerges from empirical studies and reflections attempts to distinguish three levels or steps in the development of human ethics. The first level has to do with the individualistically oriented ethic based on principled attitudes. This ethic relates to the small group problems, is functional in 'face-to-face' relationships and is summarized by the Ten Commandments of the Decalog. The second level of the development of ethics—the socially oriented one —does not neglect the face-to-face relation but additionally and above all stresses the ethical effect of *the role* of the individual and the institution in which this individual is entangled, in the broader social area. This type of ethic is oriented toward social justice. Different notions of social justice and the clash of different social Weltanschauungen, and the disputes and fights which they trigger among different ideologies, generates a need for a more general ethic which constitutes the third phase of development.

This is *the global ethic*. It says that the earth is the only and the common home for different social systems; even more, for all living beings. This is because the global ethic embraces not only the diversity of different social systems, and the relation of these systems to the environment, but also the relation of mankind to all other living creatures. The global ethic, paradoxically enough, stresses—when it deals with population growth, human resources, environment—the problems which until recently were regarded as entirely economic, technical, demographic ones. Thus, as it is possible to say that the main goal of the individually oriented ethic is that of the smoothing of relations among people and attainment of the dignity of man, and as it is possible to say that the socially oriented ethic strives to establish the canons of social justice, so it might be said that the global ethic is oriented toward the creation and preservation of the unity of all living creatures. The global ethic extends the features of the individual code of norms through the structure of social orientation into a general perspective: so, according to this ethic, everybody should be regarded as a reliable tutor of dignity and justice not only for those whom he meets in 'face-to-face' relations and not only for those whom his social role or position might indirectly affect, but also those with whom he is entangled in the net of interrelations —constituted by life—which influence the resources of the life itself.

part three

Conclusions

8 Values and realization: the equation of the ideal and the real

The role of value judgments in the practical sciences

It has been asserted that the practical sciences cannot be recognized as objective disciplines inasmuch as they make use of value judgments which are essentially subjective, and in consequence the practical disciplines become subjective ventures. We thus have to consider the extent to which value judgments actually do play a role in the practical sciences, and of what this role consists.

According to the definition accepted in previous chapters, a practical science is made up of sets of propositions detailing information on how postulated states of affairs can be realized on the basis of a description of the actual state of affairs, accepted valuations, and a knowledge of the relationships between relevant phenomena. Given this definition, there are several phases characteristic of practical procedures, such as description of the actual state of affairs and its evaluation, description and evaluation of the intended effects, description and evaluation of the projects or designs, evaluation of the gains and losses related to the change of the actual state of affairs commensurate to the cost of realizing the project, description and evaluation of the results. We can see, therefore, that evaluations do play a considerable role within the practical disciplines and thus our problem is reduced to the question of whether these evaluations deprive the practical disciplines of objective status.

As noted in chapter 1, essentially two types of evaluations can be distinguished: valuations proper and utilitarian evaluations. The latter can be classified according to three types of criteria: (a) with reference to their characteristic terms or phrases; (b) with reference to what they concern (means, ends); (c) with reference to their place in systems of values (justified vs. justifying values). In discussing the role of evaluations in the practical sciences, it is essential to indicate not only which phase of the procedure the evaluation occurs in but also in which form it appears.

The initial phase is the description of the existing state of affairs and its evaluation. In this phase, we obviously have value judgments. They appear from the very outset, when it is determined which data should be included in the description, and which left out; what is evaluated is the significance of the data in the given descriptive context. However, it can easily be seen that these value judgments are utilitarian ones; the selected data are appreciated as adequate means for attaining an adequate description. The judgments are thus utilitarian evaluations of type (b). But we also have explicit value judgments such as decisions on whether the facts as described ought to be changed or not; an overall negative or positive evaluation of the whole context is established. But these value judgments, too, are utilitarian. They are arrived at on the basis of comparing them with other accepted value judgments. The description of the existing state of affairs and its evaluation are compared with the accepted valuations, and the overall evaluation is formulated as a result of the comparison. It is thus a utilitarian evaluation.

The collation of valuations, though a logically separate phase of the procedure, is sometimes done in the course of description, or of project making, or even when the results are reviewed. At this point valuations proper are involved, relating to the ends of the given practical enterprise. However, such valuations as applied to descriptions, projects, results, though they are emotive judgments, do not introduce subjective elements into the practical sciences, for they are not a part of their language but are brought in from outside. They are accepted objective data; if they are at all discussed, it is in the language of normative systems and not in the language of the practical disciplines.

Example. The Society for Applied Anthropology formulated an ethical code for anthropologists. It stipulates that[1]

> no applied anthropologist may undertake a commission on behalf of any interest, or segment, or section of a group, which anthropologically we recognize as an interrelated system of human relationships, without a specific avowal, to those on whose behalf he undertakes the task, of his intention of taking the whole into account. He should recognize also that actions taken on behalf of any such group may create crises in the system or in individual members, and that it is the duty of the applied anthropologist to point out the need for other measures, not previously included in the group's program, to provide for recovery after such crises or disturbances have occurred.

VALUES AND REALIZATION

The role of evaluations in the practical sciences can thus be compared to the role of an anthropologist intervening in a foreign culture.

The phase of project evaluation is characterized by an appearance of utilitarian judgments (of type b), for in this phase it is determined whether the intended results will be compatible with the accepted values, and whether the project is a suitable means to the realization of these results. Assessments of the existing situation are compared with assessments of the costs of realization of the project; here, too, utilitarian judgments are involved (of either type b or type c), for the

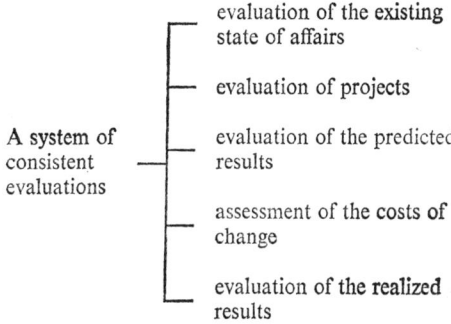

FIGURE 5

problem to be solved here is whether, considering the accepted values, the costs of realization of the intended results will remain within the limits of the overall positive results.

The last phase, or the phase of evaluation of the results, is also marked by the use of utilitarian evaluations (of type b or type c) for what is determined here is whether the results that have been brought about are in agreement with the accepted values.

The relationships between a system of values and the various situations to which the system may refer can be presented graphically as Figure 5. These considerations lead to certain general conclusions. Valuations proper occur essentially in only one phase of the research procedure in the practical sciences, i.e. in the phase of collating valuations acceptable in the pursuit of the given practical enterprise. However, those valuations are not a part of the language of the practical sciences. In all other phases of the practical procedure, utilitarian judgments only are involved. These judgments are intersubjective and do not introduce any elements of subjective arbitrariness into the practical disciplines. In other words, evaluations in the practical sciences appear either as objective data taken from outside, or as utilitarian judgments without any subjective elements in them.

CONCLUSIONS

The principle of effectiveness

The theoretical sciences aim to describe what exists and to order phenomena in terms of relevant laws. The theoretical disciplines thus aim at knowledge of the true image of reality. It is not so with the practical disciplines. Their basic aim is to study the conditions which are necessary for the realization of what is postulated. It can be said that while the ruling idea of the theoretical sciences is true knowledge, the ruling idea of the practical disciplines is knowledge which makes effective action possible.

Hence, the problem arises: What is the meaning of effective action as an ideal of the practical sciences? According to T. Kotarbiński, 'we shall call an action effective if it leads to the result intended as its aim.'[2] In accord with what has been said about purposive action, the following definition can be offered: By effective action is meant an equality between the state of affairs postulated by a purposive procedure and its results. What is involved is parity between the model on which a procedure has been based and its realization. Such a definition permits determining the degree of effectiveness of a purposive action. Namely, the degree of effectiveness of a purposive action decreases as the discrepancy between the two sides of the equation increases. An optimally effective action is that in which all the postulated elements in the state of affairs have been realized, and no other ones. An optimum of effectiveness would thus guarantee the existence of all the postulated elements and would prevent the appearance of any unintended ones. In the case of total effectiveness, we could say that the model of the purposive procedure has been completely realized.

In practice, it is impossible to guarantee all the postulated effects and to prevent any unintended effects from appearing. This is an ideal only, which can be more or less approximated. All practical activity ought to be preceded by considering to what extent the postulated aims are feasible and to what extent the available means are effective. If we know the limitations and shortcomings of the means that are at our disposal, we can predict the losses even before we have begun to act.

M. Berger summarizes the thoughts of Roscoe Pound on the limits of effectiveness of legal means in the following manner:[3]

> With the entire physical, moral, and symbolic force of the state behind it, law is truly an efficacious means to control behavior. Yet it has limitations, and there are tasks for which it is not appropriate. Roscoe Pound listed its limitations as follows: (1) The law deals with facts but we may be wrong as to what we take as facts. (2) Many duties, such as gratitude, 'morally are

of great moment but defy legal enforcement.' (3) There are
certain ways of injuring others—for example, through domestic
intrigue—which are difficult for law to restrain effectively. (4)
Many injuries—for example, to one's feelings and mental
health—cannot be prevented or adequately remedied by law.
(5) In important phases of law enforcement it is still necessary
for individuals to set the legal machinery in motion, and
individuals are often loath to do so.

The above considerations suggest a number of generalizations concerning methodological directives for enhancing the effectiveness of action. Three basic and six detailed directives can be proposed. All are related to the essential praxeological directive of the economization of action.[4]

1   Prepare an adequate description of:
    (a) diagnosed states of affairs
    (b) postulated states of affairs
    (c) results
2   Consult recognized values with reference to:
    (a) diagnosed states of affairs
    (b) prognosis
    (c) results
3   Secure empirical verification of hypotheses.

The basic directive of adequate description postulates such an empirical description of the existing state of affairs as will enable its change and the control of that change. The detailed directives for description (a) make possible the proper evaluation of the existing situation and a decision on whether it should be changed, (b) provide a design for the project that will yield hypotheses leading to its realization, and (c) permit a proper evaluation of the results of the action. The essence of the remark of one of the directors of the American Telephone Company is: In the advertising section we are shooting at a rapidly moving target. This target is never at rest. We hope to obtain three types of information by research: (1) exact knowledge on where the target actually is and in what direction it moves; (2) what ammunition should be used to hit it; (3) some indices to show us what results we have achieved.[5]

The basic directive of consulting the recognized values ensures taking into account all the valuations indispensable to assessing the existing state of affairs, to justifying the decision for change, and to evaluating the results that are eventually attained. The detailed directives for referring to recognized values (a) focus on a comparison of what is and what it is thought ought to be, (b) weigh the expected positive gains from the change as against the negative evaluation of the existing situation and possibly of the changed situation, and (c) permit determining whether the positively valued effects of the purposive procedures have indeed been attained.

The basic directive of empirical verification of hypotheses postulates an experimental and adequate justification of the hypotheses. This directive is no different from the principles that apply in the theoretical sciences.

The above methodological directives are not, as should be clear, infallible. The fallible character of methodological directives in the practical sciences has as one of its sources the fact that the directive of empirical verification of hypotheses entails only a limited justification. Another is that our empirical knowledge is by no means complete. It happens often that a procedure in accord with the directives will lead to full realization of the intended results; and yet these results may in turn bring about some unintended ones which are negative and which had not been known at the time of undertaking the project and could not possibly have been predicted. For example, streptomycine has been an effective medicine against many diseases: yet in some cases its side effects (deafness, skin disease, etc.) turn out to overbalance the advantages of its use.

Even more conducive to fallibility than the hypotheses based on analysis of empirical data are the complex phases of comparisons of evaluations and descriptions, and the prognoses and evaluations concerning realization of the postulated states of affairs. The methodological directives of the practical sciences do not afford the feeling of certainty that marks the formal sciences, based as they are on tautologies. They also fail to offer the degree of certainty characteristic of some of the theoretical sciences, based on extensive experimenting. However, this does not mean we should give up any attempts at methodological precision in the practical disciplines, which in so far as it is successful will increase the degree of effectiveness of action.

When we consider the methodological problems of the practical sciences, reflections on their relationship to the methods of praxeology[6] inevitably arise. It seems that two attitudes can be distinguished here. On the one hand, it is argued that the methodology of the practical sciences is a peculiar development of the basic praxeological principle of economization of action. On the other, it is held that the methodology of the practical sciences is some general scheme for arriving at intended results, while praxeology offers the rules on how within some general scheme its aims can be attained in the most effective manner. While both positions can be plausibly supported, especially inasmuch as they are not mutually exclusive, a detailed discussion of this issue would step beyond the scope of the present work.

Considerations of the basic problems of the practical sciences and their effectiveness lead to what may seem a paradoxical conclusion. For it can be argued, on the ground of these considerations, that the practical sciences are a certain variety of the theoretical sciences. Such a conclusion, however, would lead in turn to abandonment of the classification of sciences accepted at the beginning of this book. Instead of classifying the sciences into theoretical disciplines and practical disciplines as two distinctive classes, we would be distinguishing among the sciences (all of which would be theoretical from this point of view) those which make use of evaluations and those which do not. Of course, the sciences which make use of evaluations can indeed be called practical, but in keeping the name we should not let the word impress us to the point of considering these disciplines as non-theoretical.

The practical disciplines do take account of evaluations, but they do not themselves evaluate. They make use of evaluations, but they do not discuss them or employ them in discussion. They take them for granted as assumptions that must be acknowledged. The peculiarity of the practical disciplines consists in that they make use of descriptive and evaluative propositions, but both are handled as something given, as cards in the deck to be played with. A doctor does not dispute the judgment of his patient who (having been informed of the options) agrees or refuses to agree to any operation. He acknowledges the decision and abides by it. However, though discussions of the ultimate justifications of value judgments are placed outside the scope of scientific discourse, the problem of the validity of values is by no means meaningless. On the contrary, its import is enormous. Still, it is doubtful if it can be scientifically solved at all. What seems to be required is philosophical wisdom.

Apparently, if we classify the sciences by the kinds of propositions on which they are based, we cannot demand too strict methodological standards from the practical disciplines. Moreover, the theoretical sciences also employ evaluations; these are utilitarian evaluations as, for example, when it is decided that among the multitude of empirical data some ought to be considered and others are unimportant. If, then, we accept the character of the basic propositions as the criterion of classification of the sciences, we can discern three groups of discourses. The first group contains mainly theoretical propositions; the second contains theoretical and evaluative propositions; the third contains mainly evaluative propositions. The first group encompasses the theoretical sciences in the strict sense of the term; the second the practical sciences; the third the various systems of values. The objective and intersubjective character of the first and second groups permits recognizing them as scientific. The subjective character of the third rules it out as being such.

CONCLUSIONS

The distinction that is sometimes made between the so-called level of substance and norm ('is' and 'ought to be') can be transcribed into a distinction between descriptive and evaluative propositions. In accord with the definition of the practical sciences, these formulate postulates and prescriptions for action. They are thus a source of rules or instructions, informing as to how we should guide our conduct to attain the intended results. However, we know that if we distinguish between what is and what ought to be, no postulates are thereby entailed. What ought to be does not follow from what is. No description, however detailed, leads directly to any directive. We can try to predict what will be on the ground of a description of what is, but we cannot give any instructions. Directives become possible only on the ground of a peculiar conjunction of two elements: a description and a system of values. Pure description or a system of values alone does not permit establishing any rules for conduct. The two elements must be combined for such rules to be at all possible. From the same description different postulates can follow, when the scales of accepted values are different. Two persons may agree that the day is hot, but the person who believes that heat should be avoided will be apt to seek shelter in a cool room, while the person who believes that heat should be enjoyed will likely go to the beach. On the other hand, subjectivity and semantics can lead to differing descriptions even when similar valuations are expressed. Thus two people may agree that warm weather is pleasant, but one will say the day is 'hot' while the other says it is 'pleasantly warm'— and each will act accordingly. The solution of this paradoxically spurious contradiction was proposed at the beginning of this book.

Failure to make this kind of heuristic distinction leads the theoretical sciences to make demands on the practical disciplines that cannot be met for methodological reasons. For as R. S. Lynd has observed:[7]

> Nature may be neutral. The sun and lightning descend upon the just and upon the unjust. But culture is not neutral, because culture is interested in personalities in action. The social scientist's reason for urging the neutrality of science in such a world of bias is understandable, but it has unfortunate results that curtail heavily the capacity of social science to do precisely the thing that it is the responsibility of social science to do.

When we consider the methodology of the practical sciences we should also note that through their practice they have continually enriched the store of experience, mainly through their persistent attempts to master nature. It was reflections based on these attempts that led to the further development of the natural disciplines. This, in turn, gave impetus to the practical sciences based on them, thereby making nature more and more vulnerable to skillful human handling. Underlying the growth and perfection of the practical disciplines dependent on the theoretical natural sciences have been the experimental methods.

In the theoretical social sciences the pattern of development has been different. Experiment has, unfortunately, little application in them, and the inductions on which theoretical generalizations are based are rather limited. In such a situation, the practical sciences having to rely on the thin generalizations of their theoretical counterparts are subject to the risk of extensive errors resulting from faulty hypotheses. In the theoretical natural sciences the sequence of reinforcement is: practical sciences → theoretical sciences → practical sciences; in the theoretical social sciences the sequence is simply theoretical sciences → practical sciences. Inasmuch as empirical control is lacking, the scope of arbitrary assumptions is hardly limited at all. This fact contributes to the permanent crisis of the social sciences. It would seem, then, that continued development of the methodology of the practical social sciences, if fed back to the development of the theoretical sciences, could lead to emergence of a body of verified generalizations in the social disciplines.

Thus theoretical knowledge in the societal field would be enriched not only by the autonomous development of the relevant disciplines relying for the most part on the intellectual curiosity of scholars, but by hypotheses called forth by social needs and verified by methodologically sensitive practice. The development of the methodology of the practical sciences would thus increase the fund of social knowledge by systematically accumulating justified hypotheses. Such an empirical advance might ultimately make rational social reconstruction possible. Not only a rational but also a socially-just reconstruction.

9 Methodology of the practical social sciences and social engineering

You glorify Nature and meditate on her;
Why not domesticate her and regulate her?
You obey Nature and sing her praises;
Why not control her course and use it?
You look on the seasons with reverence and await them;
Why not respond to them by seasonal activities?
You depend on things and marvel at them;
Why not unfold your own abilities and transform them?
You meditate on what makes a thing a thing;
Why not so order things that you do not waste them?
You vainly seek into the causes of things;
Why not appropriate and enjoy what they produce?
Therefore I say—To neglect man and speculate on Nature
Is to misunderstand the faces of the universe.
                    Hsün Yzu (third century B.C.)
              See J. Needham, *Science and Civilisation in
              China* (Cambridge University Press, 1956),
                                              II, p. 28

Problem

The theoretical social sciences deal predominantly with two basic issues: the description of social reality and its explanation. These they pursue through historical inquiry, intellectual understanding, inferences from causality or indeterminism, the logical character of scientific law, functionalism, structuralism.[1] All these and similar concepts try to perceive social reality in approximation to its true 'nature.' Common sense, without the equipment available to the social sciences, also tries to grasp the sense of social reality. But there is a gap between the social sciences and their potentialities and the perceptivity of common sense. Common sense, in principle accessible to everybody, is based on identifiable authority, gives immediate answers, and is expressed in plain language. Such features do not necessarily apply to the social sciences. Still, the gap between the social sciences and common wisdom is not necessarily a void. Elements of professional knowledge link them. Professional knowledge accumulates certain amounts and types of experience and therefore supersedes common sense, which is not specialized enough. Nevertheless, a scientific approach reaches beyond professional knowledge because of its intersubjective validity. It is quite interesting to note that the more abstract, more intersubjective, more accessible to empirical test and proof the matter is, the more it is covered and penetrated by the social sciences.

But, at the same time, the farther that analyzed matter moves into the area of the social sciences, the farther removed it becomes from the yielding kind of reliable practical recommendations that common sense is so lavish in furnishing. Professional knowledge, quite often, can be used for recommendations, and for gaining advantages—cognitive and pecuniary. How does one explain this? One explanation might be that the theoretical social sciences have been able to develop a methodology all their own. This cannot be said for the practical social sciences which, according to the principle of the division of labor, are charged with preparing practical, reliable instructions. But, as it happens, the very existence of a practical social science might be open to question, and therefore its practical implications put in doubt. This is not the case with the practical natural sciences. They exist without question and their directives function quite effectively: witness, for example, medicine, agriculture, architecture, electronics, dentistry. So what, if any, are the basic features of the methodology of practical social science?

Cognitive background of the social sciences

There is some developmental and empirical evidence supporting the thesis (although not directly) that certain biological conditions, created by evolution, generate a need for cognitive explanation.[2]

> During entire aeons a man's lot was identical with that of the group, of the tribe he belonged to and outside of which he could not survive. The tribe, for its part, was able to survive and defend itself only through its cohesion. Whence the extreme force of inward coercion exerted by the laws that organized and guaranteed this cohesion? A man might perhaps infringe them: it is not likely that any men ever dreamed of denying them.

Given the immense selective importance such social structures perforce assumed over such vast stretches of time, it is difficult not to believe that they must have made themselves felt upon genetic evolution of the innate categories of the human brain— this evolution must not only have facilitated acceptance of the tribal law, but created *need* for the mythical explanation which gave it foundation and sovereignty.[3]

This point of view is probably well taken. If the need for mythical explanation of reality is biologically grounded, then the sciences, and especially social sciences, must have an urgent 'desire' to liberate their own cognitive powers from alien, illogical, irrational, misleading elements. Thus the highly developed methodology of the theoretical sciences (and to some extent also of the social sciences) might be regarded as a reflection of this tendency. It would then become quite clear that the important, basic methodological notions are intended to purify existing concepts and to release them from the heavy burden of all possible rationalizations.

Do the practical social sciences have a similar background that could be traced as a product of adaptive biological and social evolution? Without attempting to arrive at a final solution to such a question let us at least consider some relevant studies.

Recent Polish inquiries in the area of the sociology of law and social psychology have shown quite convincingly that the theoretical distinction between principled and instrumental attitudes (the autotelic and the heterotelic points of view) could be empirically distinguished, and that these two types of attitudes are correlated with different types of personality and social variables. The 'principled attitude' is defined as direct spontaneous acceptance or negation of certain rules relative to hypothetical or actual behavior. The 'instrumental attitude,' according to the proposed definition, is one of acceptance or negation of hypothetical or actual behavior being dependent upon specific consideration and calculation of different possible alternatives of behavior and the evaluation of their effects. To summarize the results of the inquiry briefly, the principled attitudes are statistically correlated with the following features: relatively older age, relative decrease in educational level, leadership position, being a qualified worker or craftsman (versus white collar workers, who are oriented toward compromise), good psychological adjustment. The instrumental attitudes are correlated with: relatively younger age, increase of the level of education, subordinative position, insecurity, and lack of good life adjustment.[4]

A somewhat similar study[5] (initiated in 1954; results published in 1970) presents—in an elaborate way—a synthesis of several more detailed inquiries. The essence of the study consists of an analysis of so-called Machiavellian attitudes. It was found that such a psychological dimension might be identified, operationally defined, and studied. The findings show that MACHs (individuals who might be regarded as Machiavellian in their attitudes toward life) are: more manipulative, less persuadable, win more often, less likely to become emotionally involved, susceptible to sheer social pressure urging compliance, cooperation and attitude change, preferred as partners, chosen and identified as leaders.

Another inquiry[6] distinguished four basic styles of leadership:

(1) The dependent leader relies on the directives and support of the top management; he is alert to rules and regulations, adheres to established practices and sees himself primarily as one who carries out the decisions made by supervisors. (2) The self-sufficient leader relies on his own knowledge and authority. He is willing to disregard higher authority and established rules if they seem inappropriate to the immediate problem; he runs his own shop in his own way and believes he should have considerable freedom. (3) The manipulative leader depends upon individual contact in getting the work done and a flexible approach to the handling of supervisory problems. He sees his task as getting people to do things his way by persuasion and influence. (4) The integrative leader uses a 'democratic' approach to the solution of problems, with reliance on informal, free communication and agreement rather than on rules or his own knowledge and authority. He sees his job primarily as one of coordination and resolving problems of communication and understanding.

All the above-mentioned studies share, among other things, one important feature: they all assume that individuals possess certain characteristics which confer the ability to act in an efficient, rational, planned way. The results of the studies indeed validate to some extent assumptions which intend to distinguish theoretical and practical backgrounds for human knowledge. So, it could be hypothesized with some fairness that in so far as individuals have an independent drive toward curiosity, search and recognition (which, at a certain stage of development, is transformed into a theoretical orientation), they also have an independent drive toward efficacious, productive, and errorless actions. If this is the case, then again the question remains: why does the cognitive attitude create a highly developed theoretical superstructure, whereas the practical attitude—in the area of social and interpersonal relations—does not?

There are at least three possible explanations for this. The first points to the possible misuse of power. Machiavelli (quite often misread) presents striking examples of this point. A less visible example is Prince Shang (four centuries before Christ), a philosopher, theoretician of planned action, ruler, and the victim of forces which he himself triggered. He said: 'Farming, trade and office are the three permanent functions in a state, and these three functions give rise to six parasitic functions, which are called: care for old age, living on others, beauty, love, ambition and virtuous conduct.'[7] And also: 'If virtuous officials are employed, the people will love their own relatives, but if wicked officials are employed, the people will love the statutes.'[8] 'If the virtuous are placed in positions of evidence, transgression will remain hidden; but if the wicked are employed, crimes will be punished. In the former case the people will be stronger than the law; in the latter, the law will be stronger than the people.'[9] And finally:[10]

> Sophistry and cleverness are an aid to lawlessness; rites and music are symptoms of dissipations and license; kindness and benevolence are the foster-mother of transgressions; employment and promotion are opportunities for the rapacity of the wicked. If lawlessness is aided, it becomes current; if there are symptoms of dissipation and license, they will become the practice; if there is a foster-mother for transgressions, they will arise; if there are opportunities for the rapacity of the wicked, they will never cease.

So, it might be claimed that human engineering equipped with high potentials for action will be used not in order to promote abstract, general values, which do not have the support of passive groups, but will be preempted by those who possess the power in order to strengthen the exercise of it.

The second argument is somewhat more complicated. Its essence is that efficient social actions require a special type of preparatory learning. In order to ride a bicycle, training is necessary; so too, in order to execute power exercise in it is needed. If this is correct then it becomes evident that politicians (as those who have direct access to power) are insiders as far as experience in the use of power is concerned. They are most reluctant to share the use of their specialized knowledge. It also becomes apparent that theoreticians who deliberate about power usually discuss questions which are inherently alien to them. They are, consequently, not able to produce any reliable argumentation on how to use power: how, that is, to produce desired social events.

The third argument is quite notorious: the theoretical social sciences, despite all appearances of methodological sophistication, are not mature enough to create a basis for reliable practical recommendations; they develop excellent cognitive skills but are subject to what Robert Merton calls 'trained incapacity.'

Nevertheless, under the pressure of urgent social needs and expectations the idea and the design of prospective social engineering, social guidance, human architecture emerges slowly but persistently.

Forerunners

So as not to get involved in the interesting but somewhat historical discussion as to the origins of 'social engineering' or 'sociotechnics,'[11] I shall mention only three scholars whose influence on the self-consciousness of this new discipline of the social sciences is especially significant.

L. Petrażycki's studies[12] on legal policy as a rational instrument of social change, though devoted to only one aspect of the problem, contained an enormous amount of intuitions, reflections, historical and legal evidence which were (and are) pertinent to the question of the adequate foundation of social engineering. The main point raised by Petrażycki was: Under what conditions and to what extent does the law (official or intuitive) influence, support, or hinder social changes in the way the legislature intended? The law, being a product of social life and also a stimulus to its change, plays one of the most important roles among the rational devices that have an impact on social life. Let me illustrate one of Petrażycki's main points with an example. The conversion that was accomplished in Sweden in 1967 from left-hand to right-hand traffic is an almost perfect empirical illustration of the law as an agent of social change. In the study which analyzed this situation it was 'hypothesized that *a degree of compliance with certain types of laws may be obtained without the complete change of attitudes which an internalization involves.*' And also: '*According to the data presented, it is not necessary to obtain a parallel change in attitudes, knowledge, and behavior when changing internalized rules.*'[13]

The term 'social engineering' was invented, apparently, under the pressure of trying to meet urgent social needs. When Gunnar Myrdal analyzed the problem of the black minority in the United States in order to propose recommendations, he was apparently the first, in a methodologically conscious way, to use this term:[14]

> There is a common belief that the type of practical research which involves rational planning—what we have ventured to call 'social engineering'—is likely to be emotional. This is a mistake. If the value premises are sufficiently, fully, and rationally introduced, the planning of induced social change is no more emotional by itself than the planning of a bridge or the taking of a census. Even prior to the state of social engineering proper, the research technique of accounting openly for one's value premises actually de-emotionalizes research. Emotion and

irrationality in science, on the contrary, acquire their high potency precisely when valuations are kept suppressed or remain concealed in the so-called 'facts.'

And again:[15]

From the point of view of social sciences, this means, among other things, that social engineering will increasingly be demanded. Many things that for a long period have been predominantly a matter of individual adjustment will become more and more determined by political decision and public regulation. We are entering an era where fact-finding and scientific theories of causal relations will be seen as instrumental in planning controlled social change.

In a work congenial to Myrdal's book (also published in 1944; and it is quite interesting that social engineering gained a 'methodological visibility' during the Second World War when the pressure of problems—military as well as social and political—became enormous), Karl Popper wrote:[16]

The Platonic approach . . . can be described as that of *utopian engineering*, as opposed to another kind of social engineering which I consider as the only rational one and which may be described by the name of *piecemeal engineering*. . . . The piecemeal engineer will, accordingly, adopt the method of searching for, and fighting against, the greatest and most urgent evils of society, rather than searching for, and fighting for, its greatest ultimate good.

These appeals—strengthened on the one side by the urgent pressure of practical needs and the inability of the social sciences to provide efficient practical guidance and, on the other, by the relatively low level of preciseness in these sciences—resulted, paradoxically enough, not in a subsequent development of social engineering but rather in 'social quackery.' Social quackery under the flag of social engineering was successful not only in producing several unexpected negative by-products and blaming the adopted parent for them, but also, through different types of misunderstandings and misuses, in creating an active negative attitude against social engineering as a 'dirty manipulation of human souls.' So now social engineering must devise a body of relevant methods and propositions as well as take up the ungrateful job of disassociating itself from the abortive effects of social quackery.[17]

Stages of development and the teleological paradigm

At least five models of the development of social engineering should be distinguished. These are the mechanistic, clinical, interventional, holistic, and methodological models, the latter containing the scheme of a teleological paradigm intended to give a comprehensive synthesis of the course of practical action (purposive procedure).

The *mechanistic model* is the classical model of social engineering, almost a pilot model, and is simply an applied model which generally provides for the following: a body of experts is given an action or research task by an agency or a sponsor, with a request for some type of diagnosis, possibly including therapeutic, corrective, palliative or projective recommendations.[18] However, as a principle, an evaluation of the goal of the requested task is beyond the competence of the experts. According to this model it is recognized as methodologically unsound for a researcher to attempt to inject his own values into the research which, after all, was predicated on a set of sponsor or agency values. Any attempt to judge or change the sponsor's values after a given task has been accepted would not be ethical or in the long-term interest of the researcher. His only option in case of value disagreement is to refuse the research task altogether. A sponsor has—this is the basic assumption—the same right to his own values as the researcher has to his. In some cases, various sponsor values may appear to be conflicting, either because they are not clearly specified or recognized, or because they are on different levels of generality. It may then become necessary for the researcher to point out such inconsistencies to the sponsor, and perhaps to help the sponsor eliminate them. However, here too the last word belongs to the sponsor. Only the sponsor or sponsoring agency is competent to judge whether a new or modified set of values is acceptable. The mechanistic model is also quite interesting from the point of view of methodological properties. According to the assumptions of this model the expert's main task is to translate theoretical propositions into teleological statements. So, the relationship between two or more variables should be transformed into a specific recommendation. There are two basic possibilities: (1) If there is an existing body of propositions relevant to the nature of the given task, the researcher's main problem is to select the especially valid ones, translate them into teleological recommendations, and combine them in a comprehensive plan of action. (2) If relevant propositions are not available, the researcher has to conduct an independent inquiry to discover the regularities that are strategically important in the given area. The second alternative is more complicated, which is a disadvantage. But the first one also has shortcomings: the preexisting propositions, usually of a general character, are not necessarily applicable to the particular set of circumstances that are the target of practical action.

The *clinical model* of social engineering is described by Alvin Gouldner[19] as a model whereby the researcher plays a much more active role than in the 'classical model.' Three basic features characterize this model and differentiate it from the classical. First, the clinically oriented social engineer not only considers the problems brought to him in need of solution, analysis, or enlightenment; he also prepares his own diagnosis of the sponsor's situation. Such a diagnosis may very well be different from the sponsor's idea, as it may be constructed partly with elements unknown to the sponsor. Second, the clinically oriented social engineer attempts to foresee troubles and obstacles that may appear, and tries to prepare ways and means to prevent or overcome them. Third, and especially in connection with the second feature, the clinically oriented social engineer deals with the problems of cooperation between sponsor and researcher. He focuses attention on cooperation during the process of investigation, later in respect to the interpretation of results, and finally during the process of translating the recommendations into action. The clinical model is thus almost a psychoanalytical version, but this is not the only conception. The so-called interventionist[20] variation also stresses the researcher-sponsor relationship, as portrayed in the following statement:[21]

> ... being an interventionist is an occupation built upon discrepancies resulting in challenging dilemmas. For example, how may an interventionist behave effectively with the client if the latter views the former's concept of effectiveness as being incorrect? The client is faced with a similar dilemma. How can he keep the interventionist in dialogue if the latter does not prefer the client's mode of conversing? One possibility that the interventionist may consider is to turn the dilemma into virtue and to use the dilemma as leverage for the initial interactions between himself and the clients.

What characterizes this variation of the clinical model of social engineering is that it tries to embrace the positive intuitions associated with the expectations of the truly interventional model, while still remaining within the formal boundaries of a financially and administratively maintained sponsor-researcher relationship. Both the clinical and semi-interventionalist models of social engineering are 'unconsciously' in thrall to this easily visible (almost businesslike) feature of secondary importance: the relationship between expert and sponsor.[22] Although the relationship is quite important for the accomplishment of the expertise process, nevertheless it should not screen the problem of primary importance: how to identify and manipulate the factors that will produce the desirable (and only those) results.

The third model of social engineering is the truly *interventional*. The major characteristic of this model is that it can function without a sponsor's initiative, the experts suggesting the need of research and recommendations to the appropriate agency, bureau or sponsor. During the research process (which could subsequently be sponsored by one institution or another) and during the preparation of recommendations, the set of values (eventually of the sponsoring agency) can be reformulated—or new values introduced. Researchers or research teams can, according to this model, press the sponsor (or sponsors) or even play potential and actual sponsors at both ends against the middle. Finally, the interventional model gives room for influencing a sponsor who tries to sidestep recommended directives or formally opposes their application. It provides the expert and researcher the possibility of a new approach. The classical approach is characterized by an unequal relation between the 'feudal' sponsor and the 'servilistic' or 'begging' expert. The interventional approach should in the foreseeable future generate a body of experts constituting a 'pressure group' who take into consideration professional standards and professionally accepted norms of behavior. These experts will have the knowledge to undertake the tasks urgently needing attention in the society, and will be motivated by growing awareness of their own instrumental capacities to solve problems. While this will change the picture considerably, still the dialectic interplay between the lack of 'social visibility' of the experts, the type of image they have and their supposedly reliable capacities to influence social life should not be overlooked. Until the engineering devices of the social sciences are able to overcome the bad odor of social quackery, the potential impact of the researchers and experts will be relatively low.

The *holistic model* of social engineering seems on the one hand to be quite promising, yet on the other quite futile. A holistic model offers a general system which 'aims to point out similarities in the theories of different disciplines where they exist,' and seeks 'to develop something like a "spectrum" of theories—a system of systems which may perform the function of a "gestalt" in theoretical constructions . . . .' Yet it is not clear how such a general system theory can escape the danger of emptiness: 'We always pay for generalities by sacrificing content and all we can say about practically everything is almost nothing.'[23]

Several theoretical developments are regarded as essential elements in the construction of such a theory. These are: cybernetics, information theory, game theory, decision theory, topology or relational mathematics, factor analysis, and general system theory in the narrower sense. Human engineering, being the correlate of theoretical developments in applied science, has according to this conception a direct link with its theoretical foundation, the general system theory. Thus, human engineering is understood as 'scientific adaptation of systems and especially machines in order to obtain maximum efficiency with minimum cost in money and other expenses.'[24]

According to Albert Hirschman, the essential elements of the social and economic system are 'exit' and 'voice.' 'Some customers stop buying the firm's products or some members leave the organization: this is the *exit option*.' And: 'The firm's customers or the organization's members express their dissatisfaction directly to management or to some other authority to which management is subordinate or through general protest addressed to anyone who cares to listen: this is the *voice option*.'[25] Using these elements he presents a holistic model of different types of institutions and organizations in given social systems.[26]

Organizations where both exit and voice play important roles are relatively few: the most important ones are voluntary associations of various types including, as a most important

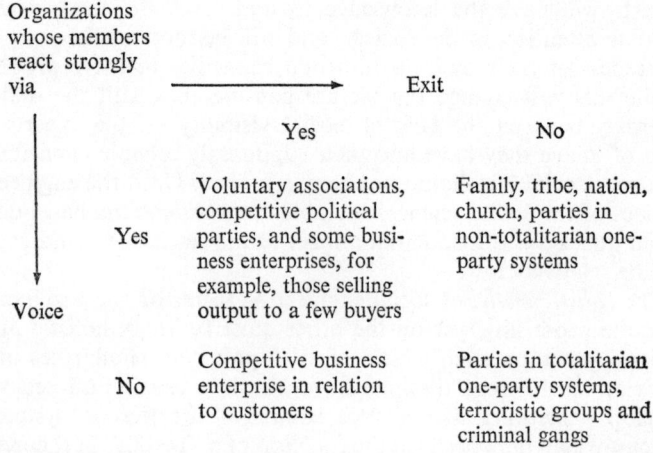

subcategory, competitive political parties. Also, certain types of clients of business firms will often attempt to influence the firms' polices directly instead of choosing exit.

There are probably no organizations that are wholly immune to either exit or voice on the part of their members....

This holistic model gives very limited information (if any at all) on how to influence firms, organizations, nations and states. The possibilities of ceasing to buy goods and of leaving organizations—and these are in reference to different categories governed by different laws—depend on so many circumstances of an economic, political, legal, social, and informational character that they do not give much homogeneous ground for finding variables which are influence-prone. The same is true for the concept of 'voice.' The prospect of abstracting from their theoretical validity any practical use of such models seems to be relatively limited. So, generally speaking, although the quest for a general, comprehensive social theory is visible (and has its voice!), still certain necessary prerequisites such as a developed body of medium level hypotheses remain indispensable for constructing a theory at a more general level.

Finally there is the *methodological model*. It is based, unlike the previous models which are more or less spontaneous and built on trial and error procedures, on methodological analysis of the peculiarities of the social sciences. The previous models primarily looked to the organizational experience of scholars who had worked in bureaux, agencies, and institutes. These were, by their nature, colored by the peculiarities of the sponsor-expert relationship. The methodological model does not neglect this type of knowledge but is nevertheless sharply aware of its limitations. The model therefore essentially rests upon a paradigm applying normative procedure to practical problems. This paradigm, once fully developed, might be used (a) as a guide on how to proceed in order to avoid possible practical errors and also (b) as a matrix which might be applied to the consecutive sequence of already performed purposeful actions in order to detect possible omissions, contradictions and errors.

The proposed paradigm is supposed to have an inherent logic. In order to discover if the planned activity under analysis is or was effective, the paradigm should be applied to all elements of the analyzed action. Inconsistencies between data describing the performed action and elements of the normative blueprint of the paradigm of this action warn against and point out where practical errors might occur. There is one thing that should be made quite clear. Just as theoretical knowledge rests upon the *adequate description of existing, empirically grasped reality,* so does practical knowledge rest upon *inherent consistency among the elements of the planned action*. Thus the basic criterion of theoretical knowledge is reliance on the perception of reality, and the basic criterion of practical knowledge is consistency with the normative plan of action. The scheme of the paradigm containing the sequence of planned action (course of teleological procedure or purposive procedure) can be summarized as in the paradigm of planned action on pp. 112–13.

This paradigm needs some explication. The seven essential steps outlined above (A-G) are necessary for performing the complete

PARADIGM OF PLANNED ACTION (teleological paradigm)

A Set of values (in hierarchical order with clear priorities)
B Diagnosis (systematic and comprehensive description—in empirical terms—of the existing situation; diagnosis in both a narrow sense and a broad sense)
C Global evaluation of the existing situation:

Equivocal		Univocal	
		negative	positive
(a) negative evaluation of the given situation from the viewpoint of a given set of values at the same time as a	(b) positive evaluation of this situation from the viewpoint of a global set of values or a different set of values	(a) negative evaluation of the given situation	(b) positive evaluation of the given situation
		(c) when prognosis tells that costs of the procedure (course) are less expensive than tolerance of the existing situation	(d) when prognosis tells that the costs of the procedure are more expensive than tolerance of the existing situation
need of suspension of the teleological course until the final evaluation is reached		need of teleological procedure	no need of teleological procedure

⎿— need of final evaluation —⎾

Conclusion / Basis for value evaluation / Preliminary Diagnosis

COURSE OF TELEOLOGICAL PROCEDURE

METHODOLOGY OF THE PRACTICAL SOCIAL SCIENCES

D Theoretical basis
  I (a) preventive (b) projective (c) corrective
  II plan (description of non-existing situations which are approved by the set of values; goals)
  III search for independent variables (genetic or causal)
  IV selection of the accessible means
  V verification of registered regularities (hypothesis)
    (a) previous research (b) new research design
  VI tentative construction of the project and evaluation of the possible consequences

E Practical decision
  VII authorization of the plans
  VIII realization of the action

F The cognitive projection of results
  IX effects (scope of the adequacy of the plan)
      intended   non-intended
      positive   positive
      positive and negative   positive and negative
      negative   negative

G Evaluation
  X evaluation of effects
  XI correction procedure (if needed)
  XII final evaluation

{ verification of teleological procedure

Final testing of hypothesis | Realization of the project | Inspection of results | Final evaluation

COURSE OF TELEOLOGICAL PROCEDURE

scheme of an action if it is to be methodologically and technically proper and if it is to provide a pattern of general efficiency.

The first step is the *classification of the values* expected to be related to the anticipated action. These values can be constructed as a clear hierarchical set or can be mixed, or even 'confused,' in their interrelationship. They can be complete or incomplete. They can be contradictory, or they can be consistent. To classify these sets of values, either an analytical or a synthetical approach is necessary. An analytical approach would be proper when the task is to construct a hierarchy of non-contradictory values, to establish priorities, to eliminate spurious contradictions, etc. A synthetic approach would be necessary when contradictions cannot be resolved analytically. Traditionally several devices have been established to achieve an order among values: elections, courts, mediations, referenda, public opinion studies, activities of professionals such as priests, politicians, ethical philosophers, etc. Let us be clear on at least one very important point: social engineering, or any planned action in the practical social sciences, can be accomplished *only* under the condition of an agreement on the basic priorities in values. Values are introduced to the language of the methodology of practical sciences from the realm of their normative meta-norms existence. But, once they are incorporated into the course of teleological procedure, they become elements of this procedure. This dual character of values leads to many mistakes and misunderstandings: at the stage of value formulation values can (and should) be evaluated, placed in proper hierarchical order, classified, modified, rejected, etc. Once accepted, they transform themselves into 'neutral' elements, variables which are (and will be) taken into consideration according to the meaning and place they have been given at the stage of value classification.[27]

The second step, *the diagnosis*, must be related to the existing social situation.[28] It should be accomplished with the use of the proper empirical and methodological techniques, should be presented in proper empirical and methodological techniques, should be presented in proper language (including also simulation models), and should clearly state the time and space limitations relative to the existing type of social system. This is the task of the diagnosis in a narrow sense. In a broader sense it should also give a tentative explanation of the interplay of the perceived causes of the existing state of affairs. This stage in the course of teleological procedure creates one of the essential links between the practical and the theoretical sciences: it utilizes all the achievements of the theoretical sciences, and at the same time takes advantage of recent methodological developments. Three types of diagnosis should be distinguished: (a) that oriented toward the past, (b) that oriented toward the existing situation, (c) that oriented toward the future.

The diagnosis oriented toward the past utilizes all data accumulated by historical disciplines with a special interest for new, emerging tendencies. The diagnosis oriented toward the future aims to anticipate in a cognitive way the main trends of the development of the existing situation. All possible types of forecasting (futurology) fall under this category.

The third step, *global evaluation of the existing situation*, utilizes the data collected in the two previous phases of the teleological procedure. Based on the information thus obtained, a decision should be reached in the form of a final statement as to whether the next stages in the procedure should be undertaken. This step will either close the course of the teleological procedure, reducing it to a short circle, or make it an extended one.

The fourth step consists in *the elaboration of the theoretical basis* for practical action. The collection and elaboration (checking the methodological acceptability of the elements in the collected body of hypotheses) of possible regulations should point to the relations between anticipated end and accessible means. It should also take into account all possible regularities gleaned from various accessible branches of the social sciences. On the basis of the data, the type of strategy chosen will be either: preventive (the main task being counteraction against 'negative' incipient tendencies); projective (the main task being to prepare and develop an entirely new plan); or the corrective (the problem being reasonable modification of already accomplished actions). The problem of modification is sometimes quite complicated; a whole new projective strategy may be required to achieve the goals that were the target of the original teleological course of action, and there is the additional task of removing the negative byproducts of the previous abortive actions. The collection and utilization of a body of hypotheses is one of the most crucial linkages in the course of practical procedure. Cherns points out an antinomy involved here: 'If, then, we conclude from all this that the more generality and hence *potential* utility the research poses, the weaker the system by which it may enter action-decision channels, we must ask ourselves whether we can improve the research-action diffusion channel or must construct a new one.'[29] On the basis of the theoretical background, several alternative strategies of action should be prepared. To evaluate these possible strategies, the potentialities of information theory (with all the computer facilities) as well as game theory might be utilized. This stage in the course of practical procedure ends with choosing the most adequate (in respect to the goal) plan of action.

The fifth step of the procedure deals with the *practical decision to carry out the plan* and the realization of its *practical (empirical) requirements*. At this point in the teleological paradigm two meta-elements enter. The first is political, ethical and psychological—i.e. the decision to undertake realization of the plan. The second is technical and physical—i.e. the task of carrying this decision into the spectrum of intended results. Again, both elements enter the teleological paradigm from another level of reality, but once they step into the logic of choices they become inherent elements of the practical procedure.

The *cognitive projection of results*, including identification of all possible effects of the performed actions, constitutes the sixth step of the practical procedure. All accessible research techniques should be used at this stage to study the whole array of accomplished and impending consequences of the implemented plan. Sociological, economic, demographic, and political inquiries can contribute a great deal toward presenting a comprehensive picture of the results. The cybernetics with feedback concept might be used to help establish a global synthesis of the effects detected.

Values open and close the practical procedure. So, as a seventh step, *the evaluation of the whole sequential performance of the teleological paradigm* terminates the course of practical procedure. The evaluation should be both partial and global. It is partial when, after the evaluation of all possible effects (unintended, unexpected, etc.), there is need of an additional corrective action. It is global when the goals of the procedure have been reached, and/or any additional action, even if desirable, would be too costly in relation to expected gains.

The teleological paradigm presented on pages 112-13 is designed to avoid the shortcomings of eclectic approaches which, even when they summarize relevant problems in a very perceptive way, are not able to bring order and hierarchy to the multiplicity of points of view. These points of view drift in different directions—examples from the existing literature can readily be found even if structured in a formally consistent style.[30]

These considerations [dealing with the scheme of global action— A.P.] can now be translated into the language of planning, as follows:

1) A plan is a complex dynamic system designed in the term of a controlling event-structure whose function is to effect its environment, which is another complex dynamic system, the kind of organized change which current values define as 'progress.'
2) The structure of the plan can be visualized as having three hierarchically related levels:
   a) An operational level at which the plan is mainly mechanistic in character;

b) A higher, strategic, level at which the plan is kinetic in character.
   c) A still higher, normative, level at which the plan is telic in character.
3) All plans fulfil their functions under two general types of control.
   a) Controls that pertain specifically to each level of their structure.
   b) Controls that emanate from the laws—both natural and human—that control the environment.

One other approach, also eclectic but mainly psychologically oriented, should be mentioned. This approach under the heading 'Proposed problem-solving paradigm' points out several issues which though belonging to different areas and methodological categories are nevertheless important. These are:[31]

1) There are great differences among humans. 2) Positive incitement is a better modifier of human behavior than punishment or threat. 3) Social problems are solved by correcting causes not symptoms. 4) Human conflict is no more inevitable than disease and can be solved or, even better, prevented. 5) Irrational feelings must be reduced before people can reason. 6) Human motivation is complex; no one does or fails to do something for only one reason. 7) Problems are solved more effectively in groups than individually. 8) Perceptions are more relevant to social problems than are 'true facts.' 9) Time and effort are not available in infinite amounts for problem-solving. 10) Responsibility for individual improvement of subordinates, students, and others, should shift largely from them to higher authorities. 11) Supervisors and teachers should receive intensive training in social science technology.

It is difficult to deny that considerable wisdom is contained in these recommendations. But it is also difficult to deny that they are insufficient to secure efficient action. If so, a meta-guidance or rule of a higher order is necessary to select or suggest those directives which are appropriate for the problem-solving mechanisms applicable to the social sciences.

Therefore the teleological paradigm is designed not only to encompass the achievements of the various eclectic approaches but also to provide a general framework for such recent methodological and theoretical developments as simultaneous technics (an element of diagnosis), forecasting (an element of extended diagnosis), information theory, game theory, decision theory (elements of a theoretical basis for evaluation of different plan-options), social sciences utilization (an element for the construction of the plan of action), cybernetics (an element of evaluation of achieved effects). A more comprehensive, precise and elaborated paradigm is obviously needed to put all these developments into the proper, methodologically interrelated stages of the global scheme of practical procedure. Nevertheless, in spite of its shortcomings, the proposed teleological paradigm tries to organize scattered and loosely connected elements into a unified pattern.

Two examples and a comment

At the end of February 1971, the Council of Ministers in Poland prepared (pursuant to the initiative of the Ministry of Justice) a new law dealing with so-called 'social parasites.' The final version of the legislative project was preceded by a relatively long and interesting public discussion through the mass media. The discussion tried to single out and analyze several social and moral values and items connected with the problem of unjustified living at the expense of society. According to the drafted proposal a 'social parasite' is a person over 18, not studying, capable of but persistently avoiding socially useful work, and gaining financial resources in a way contradictory to the basic norms of social coexistence. According to the legislative proposal, such persons should, after a complicated legal procedure whereby all the more lenient legal measures have been duly exploited, be sent to 'centers of therapy work.' So, the problem evidently belonged to the social engineering area: it was a real social problem, it had to do with several basic social values, and the diagnosis was rather clear since at least 50,000 people of this category had been identified. A need for social change was recognized, and there was a general feeling that something had to be done about it. A plan of change (the proposed law) was outlined.

Still, a group of social scientists (sociologists, lawyers, psychologists, pedagogists, etc.) were skeptical about the proposal. Almost immediately it was found that the proposed law was in disagreement with several existing laws, including international agreements. In order to find out if the attitude of the average citizen was in reality against 'social parasites,' a quick pilot study on public attitudes was conducted. The results were quite interesting. A considerable part of the population was indeed against 'social parasites' (the explanation of this being that when a social issue constitutes a new problem, *tabula rasa*, the influence of the mass media is quite effective), but the overall picture of the situation was far from clear.[32] Subsequently, a more penetrating diagnosis of the social backgrounds of the 'social parasites' was prepared. It became clear that the category was not homogeneous, for at least three different subgroups belonged to it— prostitutes, alcoholics, black market operators. It was recognized that different strategies were needed to deal with the different categories of deviants. Prostitution is legal, and educational and professional measures of social control seemed here to be most appropriate. Alcoholics need mainly medical care and social treatment—not sanctions. Black market sharks did not necessitate a new law—the existing ones covered them. Only a more efficient execution of existing laws was needed. A comprehensive memorandum which summarized these issues (and some additional ones) was submitted to Parliament (that is, to its proper committees) and after some further careful deliberation the proposed version of the law was rejected.

This example demonstrates in an abbreviated way the main but preliminary state of a social engineering procedure. As a result, because of this procedure the plan of social action (the result of interaction among the initial stages of the teleological paradigm—value consideration, diagnosis, utilization of theoretical background) was stopped before implementation. Negative results are sometimes positive.

The second example is connected with the institution of the workers' courts. A 'social court'[33] is a jury composed of a number of the employees of a company, summoned to judge various types of minor offenses committed by their colleagues, but not having real penalty competence (i.e. to impose fines or jail terms as punishment). The institution of social courts was introduced into the social and organizational life of Poland in 1960, at the beginning as a social experiment without legal recourse, and finally in 1965 as a legal possibility. The institution of social courts became, shortly after its experimental birth, an object of sociological inquiry. Thus, the interesting question arises: To what extent did sociological-legal investigations influence the content of the bill of 1965? To answer this an analysis of the mutually supplementing sociological-legal investigations and several legislative moves was undertaken.[34]

An analysis of the legislators' moves showed that they did not refer to any results of the sociological-legal investigations when elaborating the projected regulations of the bill. This indicates that legislators do not consider science as an institutionalized partner to turn to for opinions in instances where scientific research might shed light upon the problems of interest to them. Of course, the fact that these sociological-legal investigations were not referred to does not at all mean that their results were not considered by the legislators. It only means that, on the one hand, sociologists were unable to translate their results into recommendations that could be directly assimilated and accepted by the legislative agency, and on the other, that the legislators, undertaking the difficult and complicated task of giving legal shape to a new institution, might have been mainly seeking help from their traditional partners. This finding indicates that both sides, scientists and policy makers alike, ought to evolve the relevant 'relay roles,' whose task it would be to translate the results of social researches into a language familiar to the legislators, as well as to inform scientists about problems significant and vital for the lawmakers. Although such a function is now performed in some measure by administrative officials who are at the same time active scientists, it is still essential that these roles be performed systematically and within an institutional framework, rather than only by lucky coincidence. This example is meant to show not only that the relations between experts and potential sponsors are significant, but that independent of these relations the repository of theoretical propositions (usually available through the experts) is what really counts in the course of practical procedure.

The second example shows quite clearly that the resources of the social sciences were not utilized by potential sponsors at the critical stage in the teleological procedure, and that the existing theoretical fund was not capitalized upon in a proper methodological manner.

The two examples are meant to show that application of the teleological paradigm can test the methodological correctness of the existing practical procedure, and that a relevant theoretical background for this procedure is important. This background should be carefully chosen so as to avoid the mistakes 'general system theory' (GST) is inclined to make due to its level of abstractness, consequent vagueness and non-empirical orientation. Hall and Lindzey have justly stated: ' "All theories of behavior are pretty poor theories and all of them leave much to be desired in the way of scientific proof." This being said in a textbook of nearly 600 pages on *Theories of Personality*. We can therefore hardly expect GST to present solutions where personality theorists from Freud and Jung to modern writers were unable to do so.'[35] I would only add that all non-analytical theories should be based on empirical inquiries and therefore should be included in the domain covered by the empirical approach. The action-research approach selects such theories more efficiently than do abstract requirements.

Concluding remarks

Practical social sciences might be defined as a conjunction of general statements ascertaining how, on the basis of the relations between social facts, one might realize states of affairs recommended by accepted values. This definition is consistent with the notion of praxeology—the general theory of efficient action.[36] Social engineering might be regarded as a particular category of praxeology and practical sciences. It is interesting to note here that all three share the teleological paradigm in common. How can these general concepts be utilized to fulfil the main goal of practical orientation underlying all these approaches? This question is even more acute now than it was earlier.

John Platt forcibly stresses the acceleration of social changes taking place at present: 'In the last two decades, the changes have been coming faster than ever before. Planes have passed the speed of sound, bombs have become incredible and then incredible squared. Men are in orbit; and here below, new countries have proliferated, television has become universal, and every corner of the world is in a state of ferment.'[37] What should be done in order to meet the challenge of these changes?

One possible option for dealing effectively with these problems is system engineering. 'Systems engineering considers the content of the reservoir of new knowledge, then plans and participates in the action of projects and whole programs of projects leading to applications. It considers the needs of the customers and determines how these can be met in the light of all knowledge both old and new. Thus system engineering operates in the space between research and business....'[38]

System engineering, no doubt, might be a very efficient tool and instrument for introducing new social constructs more adequate to the changing social situations than those resulting from spontaneous developments. But the stress on 'research and business relations,' the insistence on those tasks visible only inside the existing social order, and the emphasis on technical requirements (research, system engineering, development, manufacture, and operation) all omit the human factor in planning social changes. The same remarks might be applied—*mutatis mutandis*—to the notion of 'human engineering.'[39] So: How do we meet the challenge of ongoing social changes? Etzioni points out who might bear this task:[40]

> In the inauthentic society the majority of the members are caught in the typical cleavage between their private selves and public roles and manage by treating their neuroses with drugs, alcohol, professional counseling, and the like, thus reinforcing the inauthenticity of the society which caused their malaise. There is a minority of retreatists who ignore their public roles and build lives around their private selves. While these people are more authentic and, potentially, carriers of societal change, they have little societal effect. Finally, there are those who evolve new public selves which they collectivize and make the basis of their societal action. In these lie the hope for an initiation of the transformation of the inauthentic society. They are the active ones.

It is, therefore, to these active ones that I address, if not dedicate, the thoughts in this book on how to pursue purposeful action in building a better world based on social justice, creativity, friendship, in combat with all oppressive forces.

Notes

Introduction

1 Conceptions concerning the classification of sciences are discussed by T. Kotarbiński in 'Z dziejów klasyfikacji nauk,' *Życie Nauki*, 1950, no. 3–4, p. 232; and by B. M. Kedrow, *Classification of Sciences*, Moscow, 1961.
2 K. Menger, *Untersuchungen über die Methode de Sozialwissenschaften*, Tübingen, 1883.
3 L. Petrażycki, *Nowe podstawy logiki i klasyfikacji umiejętności*, Warsaw, 1939, pp. 44ff. Petrażycki's idea was later developed by J. Lande in 'Teoria prawa. Cześć I: Wstęp metodologiczny do nauk prawnych (1929/30),' in *Studia z filozofii prawa*, Warsaw, 1959, pp. 335–401. Similar thoughts are expressed by H. Kelsen, *Society and Nature*, London, 1936.
4 A similar classification of sciences, set forth by Kazimierz Dobrowolski, is presented in a paper by G. Langrod, 'Political science in Poland,' *Contemporary Political Science*, 1950, pp. 179–84, 189–90, 192–3. After I had completed a Polish book (1962), I received from K. Dobrowolski a reprint of his paper 'Badania socjologiczne jako podbudowa działania' (Social researches as the background of action), *Sprawozdania z posiedzeń Komisji Oddziału PAN w Krakowie*, January–June 1960, pp. 1–14. It contains many interesting thoughts concerning the practical sciences and their role.
5 W. Biegański, *Metodyka teleologii*, Warsaw, 1910.
6 K. Krzeczkowski, *O stanowisko nauk praktycznych*, Warsaw, 1936.
7 G. Hostelet, 'L'élaboration scientifique de la notion de cause,' *Annales Scientifiques et Industrielles*, Paris, 1937; 'Les rapports entre les principes du bon travail et la méthodologie de l'investigation scientifique dans les domaines de l'action,' *Studia Philosophica*, 1951, vol. 4, p. 23; 'Aperçu sur les positions de problèmes de l'action,' *Revue Philosophique*, 1952, vol. 114; 'Metodologia naukowego badania czynności ludzkich,' *Myśl Współczesna*, 1947, July–August, pp. 71–105.

8 R. K. Merton, 'The unanticipated consequences of purposive social action,' *American Sociological Review*, 1936, pp. 894–904.
9 K. Llewellyn, 'The effect of legal institutions upon economics,' *American Economic Review*, 1925, XV, no. 4, p. 671.
10 The problem is not discussed at all in the chapter, 'Methods of Social Research 1945–55,' by P. Rossi, in *Sociology in the USA*, ed H. L. Zetterberg, UNESCO, 1956. The volume summarizes the achievements of the social sciences in America during that Period.
11 Parts I–II, New York, 1951–3.
12 New York, 1951.
13 New York, 1958.
14 New York, 1957.
15 New York, 1957.
16 *Encyclopedia Britannica*, 10.
17 *Annals of Mathematical Studies*, 38, Princeton, 1956.
18 New York, 1954.
19 *Psychological Bulletin*, 1954, 5, pp. 38–417.
20 Warsaw, 1959, 2nd ed., 1961.
21 New York, 1957.
22 Chicago, 1953.
23 New York, 1957.
24 New York, 1950.
25 Princeton, 1950.
26 Cincinnati, 1959.
27 New York, 1959.
28 Chicago, 1951.
29 New York, 1937.
30 *Ethics*, 1935, 45, pp. 282–316.
31 Harvard University Press, Cambridge, Mass., 1951.
32 Durham, N.C., 1952.
33 New York, 1956.
34 London, 1949.
35 In the volume *Modern Sociological Theory*, ed. H. Becker and A. Boskoff, New York, 1957, pp. 93–133.
36 Minneapolis, 1954.
37 *Symposium of Sociological Theory*, Evanston, Illinois, 1950, p. 509.
38 *Journal of Philosophy*, 1945, XL, II, no. 8.
39 Little, Brown, Boston and Toronto, 1959.
40 Prentice-Hall, Englewood Cliffs, New Jersey, 1952.
41 Lincoln, Nebraska, 1957.
42 *Philosophy of Science*, July 1949, vol. 16, no. 3, pp. 174–5.

1 The notion of valuation

1 M. Ossowska, *Podstawy nauki o moralności*, Warsaw, 1963, p. 53.
2 Z. Ziembiński, *Normy moralne a normy prawne*, Poznań, 1963, p. 18.
3 M. Ossowska, *op. cit.*, pp. 53–4.
4 Z. Ziembiński, *op. cit.*, pp. 15–16.
5 M. Ossowska in *Kwartalnik Filozoficzny*, 6, 1946, no. 2–4, p. 279.

6 M. Ossowska, *Podstawy nauki*, p. 335.
7 It is necessary to notice that the literature on the subject of values is quite impressive, and at the same time, confusing. A comprehensive bibliography of this literature is contained in E. M. Allert, C. Kluckhorn, et al., *A Selected Bibliograph yon Values, Ethics, and Esthetics*, Free Press, Chicago, 1959.

2 What is the concern of the practical sciences?

1 J. Lande, 'Teoria prawa,' in *Studia z filozofii prawa*, Warsaw, 1959, p. 370.
2 T. Kotarbiński, *Elementy Teorii Poznania, Logiki Formalnej i Metodologii Nauk*, Wrocław, 1961, pp. 447–8.
3 Cf. pp. 58–61 below for a summary of considerations on this issue.

3 The practical natural sciences and the practical social sciences

1 R. K. Merton, *Social Theory and Social Structure*, Free Press, Chicago, 1949, pp. 163–5.

4 The course of purposive procedure

1 T. Kotarbiński, *Sprawność i błąd*, Warsaw, 1956, p. 83. According to this definition, a practical error consists in 'vain or dysfunctional motions, or cases when a motion hampering the achievement of the end has been made.'
2 *Narodowiec*, July 28, 1960, no. 177.
3 C. Sellitz, M. Jahoda, M. Deutsch, S. W. Cook, *Research Methods in Social Relations*, Dryden Press, New York, 1954, vol. I, pp. 53f.
4 G. Sjoberg and L. D. Cain, 'Negative values and social action,' *Alpha Kappa Delta, Sociological Journal*, 1959, Winter, pp. 63–70.
5 M. Ossowska, 'Ocena i opis,' *Kwartalnik Filozoficzny*, 1938, vol. XIV, no. 4, pp. 273–95; J. Lande, 'O ocenach. Uwagi dyskusyjne (1948),' in *Studia z filozofii prawa*, Warsaw, 1959, pp. 729–841 (includes a bibliography on pp. 840–1).
6 J. Cohen, R. A. H. Robson and A. Bates, *Parental Authority: The Community and the Law*, Rutgers University Press, New Brunswick New Jersey, 1958.
7 *Ibid.*, p. 12.
8 *Ibid.*, p. 195.
9 *Ibid.*, p. 80.
10 *Ibid.*
11 Observation of real cases suggests proposing the following distinction. The initial diagnosis can lead to: (1) a positive evaluation of a part of the circumstances and a neutral evaluation of the others; (2) a negative evaluation of a part of the circumstances and a neutral evaluation of the others; or (3) a positive evaluation of some of the circumstances, a negative evaluation of some others, and a neutral evaluation of the rest. The latter is the case when states of affairs are evaluated which are not subject to description from the point of view of the relevant

values. For example, if the objective of a purposive procedure is to increase the efficiency of a lathe, an evaluation of the color of its paint as ugly is neutral from the standpoint of the selected objective. However, such a distinction (achieved by introducing the concept of a neutral value judgment) is not theoretically sound. For even in the case where all the states of affairs are either positively or negatively evaluated, there remain others which are subject to neutral evaluation, since there are always numerous states of affairs which are not evaluated at all. Such a distinction could only be useful in that it would point to the risk of too rashly dismissing some states of affairs as neutral, because of a failure to realize their significance or because some values have been neglected. The distinction might also point out that in research there is always some choice to be made and some facts must be dismissed as irrelevant.

12 F. K. Beutel, *Some Potentialities of Experimental Jurisprudence as a New Branch of Social Science*, Lincoln, Nebraska, 1957, p. 198.
13 *Ibid.*, p. 125.
4 C. Sellitz, M. Jahoda, M. Deutsch and S. W. Cook, *op. cit.*

5 Elements of projective procedure

1 By a hypothesis we mean here a conjecture as to a causal relationship.
2 Cf. T. Kotarbiński, *Kurs logiki dla prawników*, Warsaw, 1961, p. 132.
3 C. Czapòw and S. Manturzewski, *Niebezpieczne ulice*, Warsaw, 1961, p. 400.
4 C. Czapòw, *Czy Johnny stanie się gangsterem?*, Warsaw, 1959, p. 76.
5 L. Festinger and D. Katz, *Research Methods in the Behavioral Sciences*, New York, 1951, pp. 618–19.
6 R. K. Merton, 'The role of applied social sciences in the formation of policy,' *Philosophy of Science*, vol. 16, no. 3, July 1949, p. 171.
7 T. Sellin, *The Death Penalty*, American Law Institute, Philadelphia, 1959, p. 21.
8 S. M. Lipset, 'The Political Process in Trade Unions,' in Morroe Berger, Theodore Abel and Charles H. Page (eds), *Freedom and Control in Modern Society*, New York, 1954, pp. 84, 87, 108, 119.
9 R. K. Merton, *op. cit.*, p. 179.
10 R. K. Merton, *Social Theory and Social Structure*, Free Press, Chicago, 1949, pp. 176–8 (pp. 223–4 in the 1957 edition).
11 The elements described in a project as ways to achieve the desired states of affairs are what is commonly called 'the means.'
12 T. Kotarbiński, *Elementy Teorii Poznania* ..., Wrocław, 1961, p. 477.
13 *Ibid.*, p. 446.
14 G. L. Seidler, *Doktryny prawne imperializmu, Studia*. Warsaw, 1957, p. 171.
15 J. Mikulowski-Pomorski, 'Czy mieszkańcy ziem górskich chcą czytać prasę regionalną?,' *Zeszyty Prasoznawcze*, 1960, no. 1, p. 23.
16 In further considerations we shall have to abandon the discussion of negative intended effects. They would make the discussion much more complicated technically, without contributing anything vital.

NOTE TO PAGE 64

17 This list of variants is complete. The set contains 12 elements which formally speaking can be recombined as in Table 6.

TABLE 6

			intended						unintended		
			positive			negative			positive			negative		
all	some	none	all	some	none	all	some	none	all	some	none
1.	2.	3.	4.	5.	6.	7.	8.	9.	10.	11.	12.

Applying combinations without repetitions (Newton's symbol

$$\binom{n}{m} = \frac{n!}{m'(n-m)!},$$

with $n > m$) or Pascal's triangle, we obtain: $\binom{12}{3} = 220$ combinations.

However, a logical analysis requires that some elements be rejected. For example, we cannot talk about some and all positive or negative unintended effects. We could hardly speak about all the unintended effects, for it is not intended to bring them about; at most, some of them can be predicted. Those eventually in advance recognized, unintended effects will have been, after they are identified, all that are considered. Thus we can only speak about some unintended positive or negative effects. Some combinations of elements must also be rejected: all intended effects include some intended effects; intended negative effects were rejected earlier (see note 16 above). Thus our set of elements has been reduced to five, as in Table 7.

TABLE 7

	intended		unintended	
				partial	
all	some	none	positive	negative
1.	2.	3.	4.	5.

The number of one-element combinations: $\binom{5}{1} = 5$. The number of two-element combinations: $\binom{5}{2} = 10$. In the latter group, three combinations have been eliminated, since $\binom{3}{2} = 3$. Thus,

$$\binom{5}{2} - \binom{3}{2} = 10 - 3 = 7.$$

The number of three-element combinations: $\binom{5}{3} = 10$. In this group, too, the excluded combinations must be subtracted. $\binom{3}{2} = 1$ and $\binom{4}{2} = 6$. Thus we have: $\binom{5}{3} - \binom{3}{3} - \binom{4}{2} = 10 - 1 - 6 = 3$. The total number of combinations: $5 + 7 + 3 = 15$. Some of these again are eliminated, for they are repeated in the one-, two- and three-element combinations. There are three such cases. Thus, the final result is $15 - 3 = 12$. The author is grateful to Mr Jan Steczkowski, Ph.D., for the mathematics.

18 Walter Gellhorn, *Individual Freedom and Governmental Restraints*, Louisiana State University Press, Baton Rouge, 1956, p. 56.
19 *Ibid.*, p. 68.

6 The corrective and preventive procedures

1 J. Kubin, 'Niektóre czynniki warunkujące skuteczność masowego oddziatywania,' *Studia Socjologiczne*, 1961, no. 1, p. 181.
2 Thus all actions designed to prevent in advance the appearance of possible or likely undesirable effects must be treated as belonging to the preventive procedure.
3 Going beyond purely methodological considerations, we can say that the preventive procedure, even though it may be most firmly based on rational assumptions, is related to an attitude of uncertainty, doubt, anxiety about the future. The projective and corrective procedures are related to the attitudes of confidence, satisfaction with what is, affirmation of the existing situation as long as it can be tolerated.
4 H. Zeisel, H. Kalven, Jr and B. Buchholz, *Delay in the Court*, Little, Brown, Boston and Toronto, 1959, p. 4.
5 H. Greenwald, *The Call Girl, a Social and Psychoanalytical Study* Ballantine Books, New York, 1958, p. 62.

7 The analytic–normative reasoning process

1 W. A. R. Leys, *Ethics for Policy Decisions*, Prentice-Hall, Englewood Cliffs, New Jersey, 1952, p. 318.
2 R. K. White, 'Value analysis: a quantitative method for describing qualitative data,' *Journal of Social Psychology*, 1944, no. 19, pp. 351–8 (as quoted by C. Sellitz, M. Jahoda, M. Deutsch and S. W. Cook, *Research Methods in Social Relations*, Dryden Press, New York, 1954, vol. I, p. 244).
3 L. P. Crespi, 'Attitudes towards conscientious objectors and some of their psychological correlates,' *Journal of Psychology*, 1944, *18*, pp. 81–117.
4 C. Sellitz, M. Jahoda, M. Deutsch, S. W. Cook, *op. cit.*, vol. II, p. 685.

5 R. S. Lynd, *Knowledge For What?*, Princeton University Press, 1939, pp. 60–2.

8 Values and realization: the equation of the ideal and the real

1 'Code of Ethics of the Society for Applied Anthropology,' *Human Organization*, ed. Eliot D. Chapple, New York, 1951, vol. 10, no. 2, p. 32.
2 T. Kotarbiński, *Traktat o dobrej robocie*, Łódź, 1958, p. 16.
3 M. Berger, *Equality by Statute*, Columbia University Press, New York, 1952, pp. 170–1.
4 This directive tells how to make actions more economic, 'either less wasteful or more efficient.' T. Kotarbiński, *op. cit.*, p. 146.
5 R. K. Merton and E. C. Devereux, 'The Role of Social Research in Public Administration,' Part I, p. 13 (unpublished).
6 T. Kotarbiński, *Praxiology*, Pergamon Press, Oxford and PWN, Warsaw, 1965.
7 R. S. Lynd, *Knowledge for What?*, Princeton University Press, 1939, p. 182.

9 Methodology of the practical social sciences and social engineering

1 E. Nagel, *The Structure of Science*, Harcourt, Brace & World, New York, 1961.
2 D. Elkind and J. H. Flavell, *Studies in Cognitive Development*, New York, 1969; also a quite detailed study on pigeons and their attitudes towards information, G. Bower, J. McLean and J. Meacham, 'The value of knowing when reinforcement is due,' *Journal of Comparative and Physiological Psychology*, 62, 1966.
3 J. Monod, *Chance and Necessity*, Alfred H. Knopf, New York, 1971, pp. 166–7.
4 A. Podgórecki, 'The categoric and teleological attitudes,' *Archivum Juridicum Cracoviense*, vol. II, 1969.
5 R. Christie and F. L. Geis, *Studies in Machiavellianism*, Academic Press, New York, 1970.
6 S. Seashore, 'The Training of Leaders for Effective Human Relations,' in R. Lickert and S. Kayer (eds), *Some Applications of Behavioral Research*, UNESCO, 1957, pp. 92–3.
7 *The Book of Lord Shang* (translated by J. J. L. Duyvendal), London, 1928, p. 197.
8 *Ibid.*, p. 207.
9 *Ibid.*
10 *Ibid.*, p. 206.
11 A. Podgórecki, 'The beginning and development of sociotechnique,' *Actes du XIe Congrès International d'Historei des Sciences XIIe section*, pp. 233–6.
12 L. Petrażycki, *Lehre vom Einkommen*, Berlin, 1893–5, and 'Predislowie wwendenie w Nauku Politiki Prawa,' *Kijewska Universiteckaja Jzwiestia*, 1896.

NOTES TO PAGES 105–8

13 Britt-Mari Persson-Blegvad and Jette Møller Nielsen, 'Law as a Means of Social Change. A Case-Study,' Warna, 1970 (mimeographed material), pp. 2 and 20. Let's omit here several doubts connected with the formulation of this last hypothesis.
14 G. Myrdal (with the assistance of R. Sterner and A. Rose), *An American Dilemma*, Harpers, New York, 1944, p. 1044.
15 *Ibid.*, p. 1022.
16 K. Popper, *The Open Society and its Enemies*, Princeton University Press, 1950 (introduction written in April 1944, ad interim Copyright granted 1946), pp. 154–5.
17 In 1971 a Research Committee on Sociotechnics at the International Sociological Association was created. The term 'sociotechnics' was adopted in order, among other things, to avoid the value-laden label of the term 'social engineering.'
18 There are some essential differences between these types of recommendations. Therapeutic recommendations seek to counteract something that would happen if the recommended action were not carried out. Corrective recommendations seek to eliminate negative effects of previous actions, erroneous actions or actions with negative side effects. Palliative recommendations address themselves to symptomatic relief; projective recommendations seek to change a present state of affairs into something else—evaluated as being 'better.'
19 A. W. Gouldner and S. M. Miller (eds), *Applied Sociology: Opportunities and Problems*, Free Press, New York, 1965.
20 C. Argyris, *Intervention Theory and Method*, Addison-Wesley, Reading, Mass., 1971.
21 *Ibid.*, p. 135.
22 The same can be said of a paper prepared by P. F. Lazarsfeld and J. G. Reitz, 'Toward a Theory of Applied Sociology' (mimeographed, 1970), which to some extent summarizes the achievements of American sociology in this area. While impressive for its methodological import and richness of material, it still does not avoid the dominance of the magic circle of the sponsor-researcher relationship. It is worth noticing, for comparative purposes, that the Section on Sociotechnics of the Polish Sociological Association has, between 1965 and 1972, held ten general conferences on the subject of the theory of applied sociology and has also been able to instigate the publication of four books on this subject. The Polish studies, albeit much poorer in illustrative material, have not been ensnared in this vicious circle. Nevertheless Lazarsfeld's general remark on the theory of applied sociology should not be overlooked. He says: 'The use of any knowledge reaches into three areas of the mind: the search for truth, the skill of forecasting, and the gift to imagine a future different from the present. There will never be clear-cut rules of procedure. The best we can hope for is to sort out the different strands and to look for regularities as they are combined into cords. The more we succeed the more energy and freedom will be left for the creative and innovating element indispensable in all utilization' ('General Instruction to the Columbia-ONR Project on Uses of Sociology,' mimeographed, p. 14). The Lazarsfeld

and Reitz paper, incidentally, while it includes a comprehensive selection of the relevant literature, omits the work of W. G. Bennis, K. D. Benne and R. Chin, *The Planning of Change*, Holt, Rinehart & Winston, New York, 1969—quite important in this area.
23 W. Buckley, *Modern Systems Research for the Behavioral Scientist*, Aldine, Chicago, 1968, p. 3.
24 L. von Bertalanffy, 'General System Theory—A Critical Review,' in W. Buckley, *op. cit.*, p. 13.
25 A. O. Hirschman, *Exit, Voice, and Loyalty*, Harvard University Press, Cambridge, Mass., 1970, p. 4.
26 *Ibid.*, pp. 120–1.
27 A stubborn and narrow-minded understanding of the methodology of practical social sciences repeatedly fails to acknowledge that the use of methodology in the practical social sciences resembles the use of a surgeon's knife: it can kill or heal. The ability to use the knife according to the requirements of medicine is one thing, the decision as to the goal of its use is quite another.
28 'Social situation'—because the problem is to present the methodology of practical social sciences. Any real situation should be taken into account when the general methodology of practical social sciences is under consideration.
29 A. B. Cherns, 'Social Research and Its Diffusion,' in *Papers on Social Science Utilization*, Loughborough University of Technology, 1972, p. 21.
30 H. Ozbekhan, 'Towards Global Action,' in *The Predicament of Man*, ed. M. Goldsmith, London, 1971, points 4–22.
31 J. A. Varela, *Psychological Solutions to Social Problems*, Academic Press, New York, 1971, pp. 272–3.
32 One of the members of the study team stated: 'Neither prostitutes nor pimps are those who create social problems. There are con men, imposters, who not only work but in their work utilize the facilities of institutions and organizations at their disposal. . . . So they are legal parasites functioning in several institutions and enjoying not only their own positions but also the privileges of their institutions. Even more, they establish relations in different types of institutions, thus creating a special type of superstructure. It is possible to extend this way of thinking and say: some institutions and social entities are pathological on the whole—not only some of the people working inside. This is the main problem.' A. Podgórecki in *Gazeta Sądowa i Penitencjarna*, no. 6 (180), December 16, 1971, p. 5.
33 A. Podgórecki, *Law and Society*, Part II, Chapter 7: The Experimental Method, Routledge & Kegan Paul, London, 1974. Workers' courts have existed in Poland since 1960. They are also established in the Soviet Union, Czechoslovakia and other socialist countries.
34 J. Wasilewski, 'The Impact of Sociological Inquiries in Legislative Decisions' (in Polish; unpublished graduate thesis, Social Sciences Department, Warsaw University, 1970).
35 L. von Bertalanffy, 'General System Theory—A Critical Review,' in W. Buckley, *op. cit.*, p. 24.

36 T. Kotarbiński, *Praxiology*, Pergamon Press, Oxford and PWN, Warsaw, 1965, p. 1.
37 J. Platt, *The Step to Man*, Wiley, New York, 1966, p. 185.
38 A. Hall, *The Methodology for System Engineering*, Van Nostrand, Princeton, 1972, p. 4.
39 The concept of 'human engineering' is analyzed in a comprehensive way in E. J. McCormick, *Human Engineering*, New York, 1957. Following is the summary of his ideas (p. 20):

1. Human engineering is the adaptation of human tasks and working environment to the sensory, perceptual, mental, physical, and other attributes of human beings.

2. The two major goals of human engineering are the improvement of work and the improvement of human welfare.

3. Human progress has developed through both experience and research. The systematic processes of research frequently contribute knowledge that cannot be obtained through experience.

4. It is largely through research that the principles and practices of human engineering are being developed.

5. Research dealing with human beings is carried out with essentially the same procedures as research in other areas. The measurement of human variables, however, usually is more difficult than is the measurement of variables in the physical sciences.

6. Human-engineering research (as well as other research) requires the identification, measurement, or quantification of two types of variables: (a) independent variable (the one being studied) and (b) dependent variables (those which are studied in relation to the independent variable).

7. Research also requires the statistical analysis of data. Common statistical techniques or procedures include frequency distributions, frequency polygons, measures of central tendency, measures of variability, correlations, and tests of statistical significance.

8. Human-engineering research may be carried out either in laboratories or in work situations. There are advantages and disadvantages to both types of studies.

9. The application of human-engineering research to practical situations is primarily the responsibility of engineers and administrators.

10. The evaluation of the applications of research findings to human-engineering problems should take into account two considerations: (a) the practical significance of the results and (b) the applicability of the results of research to the specific circumstance.

40 A. Etzioni, *The Active Society*, Free Press, New York, 1968, p. 655.

Index

Administration: atrocities by, 85; bibliography, 4
Aesthetic valuation, 17–18
Agreements, 15
Alcoholics, 118–19
Altruism, 16
Ampère, A. M., 1
Analytical-normative reasoning, 42, 76–87
Anthropology, ethical code for, 92
Arbitration, 81
Aristotle, 1
Atrocities, administrative, 85
Automation, 70

Bacon, Francis, 1
Behaviour: categoric and teleological attitudes to rules of, 16; individualistic, 84; societal, contradictory assumptions in USA, 82–4; ethical regulation of, 84–7
Berger, M., 94
Biegański, W., 2
Black market operators, 118–19
'Boondoggling' neurosis, 58
Bourgeois ethic, 16–17
Bureaucracy, 54, 57–8

Categoric attitude, 16
Cement production, 68–9
Censorship, 65–6
Change: corrective procedure for, 38–40; cost of, 34–5; projective and corrective action for, 68; social, challenge of, 121, law's role in, 3, 105

Cherns, A. B., 115
Christian ethic, 17
Classification: descriptive, 30; of sciences, 1–5, 97; of values, 91–3, 114–15
Cohen, J., Robson, R. A. H., and Bates, A., 32–3
Common sense, 100–1
Comte, A., 1
Conclusions: costs of change and, 34; in purposive procedure, 28, 38–45
Conscientious objectors, 77–8
Conventions, mutual, 15–16
Corrective procedure, 38–40, 42, 44; diagnosis, 70–4, justification of, 71–4; elements of, 70; hypothesis formulation, 71, 72–4; postulation, 67, 71; projective procedure and, 67–71, 75; projects and, 74–5
Cost: of change, 34–5; of project, 60, 93
Counter-culture, 85
Court system delays, 4, 74
Crespi, L. P., 77
Cybernetics, 118

Deadline neurosis, 57
Death penalty, 53–4
Decision-making, bibliography of, 4
Decision theory, 117
Dehumanization, 85
Deindividualization, 85

Depersonalization, 85
Description: classification, 30; purposive procedure, 28–9, 30–1, evaluation and, 31, 35
Descriptive disciplines, 2
Descriptive propositions: cognitive nature of, 10–11; discrepancies between, 41–2; emotional, 11–12, 14, 18; practical sciences, 21; valuational propositions and, 9–12, 14–16
Deviation, 86
Diagnosis: corrective procedure, 70–4, justification of, 71–4; medical, 30; projective procedure, 46–7, 52, 73, justification of, 49; purposive procedure, 28–45, conclusions, 28, 38–45, description, 28–31, elements, 28, evaluation, 28, 31–7, explanation, 28, postulating, 28, 31, 40–1, 44, 61–2; social engineering, 114–15
Dobrowolski, K., 122

Education, 16
Effectiveness: directives for, 95–6; practical sciences, 91–9; principle of, 94–9
Emotional descriptive propositions, 11–12, 14, 18
Ethic: bourgeois, 16–17; Christian, 17; global, 86–7; socialist, 16
Ethical contradictions, 82–5
Ethical judgments, 84–5; revaluation of, 19
Ethical regulation of societal behaviour, 84–7
Ethics: anthropologists', 92; hierarchical pattern, 79–80; individualistic, 16–17, 84–7; socially oriented, 16–17, 84–7
Etzioni, Amitai, 121
Evaluations (*see also* Valuations): ethical, 84–5; global, 112, 115, 116; in practical sciences, 2, 20–2, 61, 91–9, 114, social, 24; in projective procedure, 59, 64–6, 93; in purposive procedure, 28, 31–7, 76–9, description and, 31, 35, discrepant, 36, 41–2, 59, 77, 80–4, 86, 98, 114, hierarchical arrangement, 31, 79–80, 112, 114, negative, 34–7, 40–2, 64, 67, 69, 73, overall, 37, 64–5, 77, positive, 33–4, 36, 64; results, 63–6, 75, 93; teleological paradigm, 116; theoretical sciences, 97; utilitarian, in natural sciences, 24, in practical sciences, 21–2, 91–3, in sociology, 21–2
Exit and voice options, 110–11
Experimental research, 56, 99
Experts, pressure groups of, 109
Explanation: projective procedure, 47–8; purposive procedure, 28

Fear in combat, 79
Feuchtwanger, Leon, 71
Forecasting, 117

Games theory, 115, 117; bibliography of, 4
General system theory, 109–10, 120
Gouldner, Alvin, 108

Hall and Lindzey, 120
Hierarchical order: ethics, 79–80; evaluations, 31, 79–80, 112, 114; laws, 79
Hirschman, Albert, 110
Hostelet, G., 2
Human engineering, 110, 131
Hypotheses, collection of, 115
Hypothesis formulation, 99; in corrective procedure, 71, 72–4; in natural sciences, 56; in practical sciences, 47–8, 56, 59; in projective procedure, 47–8, 61, 115, justification of, 49–58, 59, testing, 54–6; in purposive procedure, 28, 40–1, 44, testing, 62; in social sciences, 56

Ideal equated with reality, 91–9
Ideological battles, 84–5
Incitement, positive, 117
Individualistic behaviour, 84
Individualistic ethics, 16–17, 84–7
Information theory, 115, 117
Informers, 12–13
Intellectuals and research, 57–8

Jews in USA, 44
Judgments, *see* Evaluations; Valuations
Justification: of diagnosis, corrective procedure, 71–4, projective procedure, 49; of hypothesis in projective procedure, 49–58, 59

INDEX

Kotarbiński, T., 15, 20, 27, 94, 124
Krzeczkowski, K., 2

Lande, J., 20
Law: aims and tasks, 59–60; limitations of, 94–5; morality and, 10, 12; role in social change, 3, 105; sociology of, 102; violations of, 35–6
Laws, hierarchical order of, 79
Lazarsfeld, P.F., and Reitz, J. G., 129–30
Leadership, styles of, 103
Legal policy, corrective action preponderant in, 70
Legal sciences, valuations in, 18
Legislative action, 3, 118–20
Lem, S., 63
Lynd, R. S., 98

McCormick, E. J., 131
Machiavelli, 103
Management, bibliography of, 4
Medical diagnosis, 30
Medicine, preventive, 70–2
Menger, K., 2
Merton, R. K., 3, 5, 24, 52, 55, 57–8, 104
Metaphysics, 5
Methodology: practical sciences, 4–5, 98, 100–21, social, 10–19, 99–121; research into, 3; social engineering, 103–7, 111–18; theoretical sciences, 102; valuation and, 18
Monod, J., 101–2
Moral valuations, 17–19
Morality and law, 10, 12
Myrdal, Gunnar, 105–6
Mythology, 102

Natural sciences: hypothesis formulation in, 56; practical social sciences and, 23–4; utilitarian judgments in, 24
Needham, J., 100
Neutrality: passive, 85; of science, 98;
Normative analysis, 76–87

Objectives, empirical language for, 59–60
Ossowska, Maria, 9, 12, 17

Paradigm: of planned action, 111–118, evaluation in, 116, examples, 118–20; proposed problem-solving, 117
Parental authority, 32–3
Passive neutrality, 85
Petrażycki, L., 2, 20, 105
Piecemeal engineering, 106
Plan: definition, 116; structure, 116–17
Planned action, see Paradigm of planned action
Platt, John, 121
Policy-makers and research, 57–8
Political parties, 110
Politicians and power, 104
Politization of social sciences, 19
Popper, Karl, 106
Postulating (see also Hypothesis formulation): corrective procedure, 67, 71; projective procedure, 46–7, 67; purposive procedure, 28, 31, 40–1, 44, 61–2
Pound, R., 59–60, 94–5
Power, use of, 104
Praxeology, 96, 120
Pressure groups, expert, 109
Preventive medicine, 70, 71–2
Preventive procedure, 40, 42, 44, 68–70
Problem-solving paradigm, 117
Project: costing, 60, 93; definition, 58–9; evaluation of results, 63–6, 75, 93; formulation, 60; realization, 61, 93; testing, 61–3
Project-making, 40–1, 58–61, 74–5
Projective procedure, 42–5; corrective procedure and, 67–71, 74–75; diagnosis, 46–52, 73, justification of, 49; evaluation, 59, 64–6, 93; explanation, 47–8; hypothesis formulation, 47–8, 61, 115, justification of, 49–58, 59, testing, 54–6; postulating, 46–7, 67
Prostitution, 118–19
Psychology, social, 102–3
Purposive procedure: concept of, 27; course of, 27–45; diagnosis, 28–45, conclusions, 28, 38–45, description, 28–31; effectiveness, 94–5; evaluation in, see Evaluations; explanation, 28; hypothesis formulation (postulating),

28, 31, 40–1, 44, 61–2, testing, 62; types of, 43; undesirable results, 62–3, combinations of, 63–4, 126–7, evaluation of, 64–6
Purposive reasoning, 27

Quackery, social, 106, 109

Racial segregation in USA, 29
Rationalization, 85
Reality: ideal equated with, 91–9; three dimensions of, 15
Realization, 115–16; project, 61, 93; values and, 91–9
Reasoning: analytical-normative, 42, 76–87; purposive, 27; reductive, 47
Research: basis for projective action, 50–1; bibliography, 4; classification of problems, 5; empirical findings from, 55–6; experimental, 56, 99; hypothesis for, 53–5; intellectuals' and policy-makers' attitudes to, 57–8; methodological, 3–5; over-specification for, 52; practical sciences, 31; time factor and, 43–4
Researcher–sponsor relations, 107–109
Resocialization, 49–50
Results: cognitive projection of, 116; evaluation of, 63–6, 75, 93; undesirable, 62–6, 126–7
Rickert, 1

Sanitary regulations in Nebraska, 35–6
Sciences (*see also* Natural sciences; Social sciences): classification of, 1–5, 97; neutrality of, 98; practical, definition, 20, 22, 94, 98, descriptive propositions in, 21, effectiveness, 91–9, evaluation in, 2, 20, 61, 91–9, 114, explanation, 48, hypothesis formulation, 47–8, 56, 59, methodology, 98, 100–21, 124–5, research methods in, 31, role of value judgments in, 91–3, utilitarian judgments in, 21–2, 91–3; theoretical, and practical, 2, 4–5, 21–2, 23, 61, 97, 99, evaluation in, 97, methodology of, 102
Seashore, S., 103

Sellin, Thorsten, 53
Semantics, 98
Shang, Prince, 104
Shils and Janovitz, 68
Simultaneous technics, 117
Social change: challenge of, 121; law's role in, 3, 105
Social courts, 119
Social engineering: clinical model, 108–9; diagnosis in, 114–15; holistic model, 109–11; interventional model, 109; interventionist, 108; mechanistic model, 107–8; methodological model, 111–18; methodology of, 103–7; models of, 107; origins of, 105–6; problem-solving paradigm in, 117; stages of development, 107–118
Social parasites, 118
Social psychology, 102–3
Social quackery, 106, 109
Social sciences: cognitive background, 101–5; hypothesis formulation, 56; methodology of valuations in, 10, 19; politization of, 19; practical, definition, 120, description of, 25–87, evaluations in, 20–2, 24, methodology of, 99–121, need for, 19, practical natural sciences and, 23–4, priorities in values in, 114, uncertainty and risk in, 24; theoretical, 19, 100–1; unity of, need for, 19; utilization of, 117
Socialist ethic, 16
Socially-oriented ethics, 16–17, 84–87
Societal behaviour: contradictory assumptions in USA, 82–4; ethical regulation of, 84–7
Sociology: of law, 102; utilitarian evaluations in, 21–2
Spencer, H., 1
Sponsor–researcher relations, 107–9
Stevenson, R. L., 57
Subcultures, 86
Subjectivity, 98
Surplus gains, 62
Systems: engineering, 121; general theory, 109–10, 120

Teleological attitude, 16
Teleological disciplines, 2

INDEX

Teleological paradigm, 111–18; evaluation in, 116; examples, 118–20
Time factor and research, 43–4
Traffic control, 38–9

Uncertainty, 24
Utilitarian valuations, *see* Valuations, utilitarian
Utopian engineering, 106

Valuations (*see also* Evaluations): aesthetic, 17–18; legal sciences, 18; methodological autonomy of, 18; moral, 17–19; notion of, 9–19; practical sciences, 20–2, 24; proper, 12–13, 17, and utilitarian, 12–13, 18; reduced to utilitarian, 13–18; social sciences' methodology, 10, 19; utilitarian, 17, 18, classification of, 91–3, definition, 12–13, natural sciences, 24, practical sciences, 21–2, 91–3, and proper, 12–18, sociology, 21–2, theoretical sciences, 97
Valuational propositions: cognitive nature of, 10–11; descriptive propositions and, 9–12, 14–16; emotional, 11–12, 14, 18
Value judgments: collecting, 32, hierarchical arrangement of, 31, 79–80, 112, 114; role in practical sciences, 91–3
Values: bibliography, 4–5; classification of, 114–15; priorities in practical social sciences, 114; realization and, 91–9
Voice and exit options, 110–11

Wartime propaganda, 50–1, 68
White, R. K., 77
Windelband, 1
Wundt, 1

Ziembiński, Z., 10, 11

Routledge Social Science Series

Routledge & Kegan Paul   London and Boston
68–74 Carter Lane   London EC4V 5EL
9 Park Street   Boston   Mass 02108

Contents

International Library of Sociology 3
General Sociology 3
Foreign Classics of Sociology 4
Social Structure 4
Sociology and Politics 4
Foreign Affairs 5
Criminology 5
Social Psychology 5
Sociology of the Family 6
Social Services 7
Sociology of Education 7
Sociology of Culture 8
Sociology of Religion 9
Sociology of Art and Literature 9
Sociology of Knowledge 9
Urban Sociology 9
Rural Sociology 10
Sociology of Industry and Distribution 10
Documentary 11
Anthropology 11
Sociology and Philosophy 12
International Library of Anthropology 12
International Library of Social Policy 12
International Library of Welfare and Philosophy 13
Primary Socialization, Language and Education 13
Reports of the Institute of Community Studies 13
Reports of the Institute for Social Studies in Medical Care 14
Medicine, Illness and Society 14
Monographs in Social Theory 14
Routledge Social Science Journals 15

Authors wishing to submit manuscripts for any series in this catalogue should send them to the Social Science Editor, Routledge & Kegan Paul Ltd, 68–74 Carter Lane, London EC4V 5EL

● *Books so marked are available in paperback*
All books are in Metric Demy 8vo format (216 × 138mm approx.)

International Library of Sociology

General Editor John Rex

GENERAL SOCIOLOGY

Barnsley, J. H. The Social Reality of Ethics. *464 pp.*
Belshaw, Cyril. The Conditions of Social Performance. *An Exploratory Theory. 144 pp.*
Brown, Robert. Explanation in Social Science. *208 pp.*
● Rules and Laws in Sociology. *192 pp.*
Bruford, W. H. Chekhov and His Russia. *A Sociological Study. 244 pp.*
Cain, Maureen E. Society and the Policeman's Role. *326 pp.*
Gibson, Quentin. The Logic of Social Enquiry. *240 pp.*
Glucksmann, M. Structuralist Analysis in Contemporary Social Thought. *212 pp.*
Gurvitch, Georges. Sociology of Law. *Preface by Roscoe Pound. 264 pp.*
Hodge, H. A. Wilhelm Dilthey. *An Introduction. 184 pp.*
Homans, George C. Sentiments and Activities. *336 pp.*
Johnson, Harry M. Sociology: *a Systematic Introduction. Foreword by Robert K. Merton. 710 pp.*
Mannheim, Karl. Essays on Sociology and Social Psychology. *Edited by Paul Keckskemeti. With Editorial Note by Adolph Lowe. 344 pp.*
  Systematic Sociology: *An Introduction to the Study of Society. Edited by J. S. Erös and Professor W. A. C. Stewart. 220 pp.*
Martindale, Don. The Nature and Types of Sociological Theory. *292 pp.*
●**Maus, Heinz.** A Short History of Sociology. *234 pp.*
Mey, Harald. Field-Theory. *A Study of its Application in the Social Sciences. 352 pp.*
Myrdal, Gunnar. Value in Social Theory: *A Collection of Essays on Methodology. Edited by Paul Streeten. 332 pp.*
Ogburn, William F., and **Nimkoff, Meyer F.** A Handbook of Sociology. *Preface by Karl Mannheim. 656 pp. 46 figures. 35 tables.*
Parsons, Talcott, and **Smelser, Neil J.** Economy and Society: *A Study in the Integration of Economic and Social Theory. 362 pp.*
●**Rex, John.** Key Problems of Sociological Theory. *220 pp.*
  Discovering Sociology. *278 pp.*
  Sociology and the Demystification of the Modern World. *282 pp.*
●**Rex, John** (Ed.) Approaches to Sociology. *Contributions by Peter Abell, Frank Bechhofer, Basil Bernstein, Ronald Fletcher, David Frisby, Miriam Glucksmann, Peter Lassman, Herminio Martins, John Rex, Roland Robertson, John Westergaard and Jock Young. 302 pp.*
Rigby, A. Alternative Realities. *352 pp.*
Roche, M. Phenomenology, Language and the Social Sciences. *374 pp.*
Sahay, A. Sociological Analysis. *220 pp.*
Urry, John. Reference Groups and the Theory of Revolution. *244 pp.*
Weinberg, E. Development of Sociology in the Soviet Union. *173 pp.*

INTERNATIONAL LIBRARY OF SOCIOLOGY

FOREIGN CLASSICS OF SOCIOLOGY

●**Durkheim, Emile.** Suicide. *A Study in Sociology*. Edited and with an Introduction by George Simpson. *404 pp.*
  Professional Ethics and Civic Morals. Translated by Cornelia Brookfield. *288 pp.*
●**Gerth, H. H.,** and **Mills, C. Wright.** From Max Weber: *Essays in Sociology. 502 pp.*
●**Tönnies, Ferdinand.** Community and Association. (*Gemeinschaft und Gesellschaft.*) Translated and Supplemented by Charles P. Loomis. Foreword by Pitirim A. Sorokin. *334 pp.*

SOCIAL STRUCTURE

Andreski, Stanislav. Military Organization and Society. *Foreword by Professor A. R. Radcliffe-Brown. 226 pp. 1 folder.*
Coontz, Sydney H. Population Theories and the Economic Interpretation. *202 pp.*
Coser, Lewis. The Functions of Social Conflict. *204 pp.*
Dickie-Clark, H. F. Marginal Situation: *A Sociological Study of a Coloured Group. 240 pp. 11 tables.*
Glaser, Barney, and **Strauss, Anselm L.** Status Passage. *A Formal Theory. 208 pp.*
Glass, D. V. (Ed.) Social Mobility in Britain. *Contributions by J. Berent, T. Bottomore, R. C. Chambers, J. Floud, D. V. Glass, J. R. Hall, H. T. Himmelweit, R. K. Kelsall, F. M. Martin, C. A. Moser, R. Mukherjee, and W. Ziegel. 420 pp.*
Jones, Garth N. Planned Organizational Change: *An Exploratory Study Using an Empirical Approach. 268 pp.*
Kelsall, R. K. Higher Civil Servants in Britain: *From 1870 to the Present Day. 268 pp. 31 tables.*
König, René. The Community. *232 pp. Illustrated.*
●**Lawton, Denis.** Social Class, Language and Education. *192 pp.*
McLeish, John. The Theory of Social Change: *Four Views Considered. 128 pp.*
Marsh, David C. The Changing Social Structure of England and Wales, 1871-1961. *288 pp.*
Mouzelis, Nicos. Organization and Bureaucracy. *An Analysis of Modern Theories. 240 pp.*
Mulkay, M. J. Functionalism, Exchange and Theoretical Strategy. *272 pp.*
Ossowski, Stanislaw. Class Structure in the Social Consciousness. *210 pp.*
Podgórecki, Adam. Law and Society. *About 300 pp.*

SOCIOLOGY AND POLITICS

Acton, T. A. Gypsy Politics and Social Change. *316 pp.*
Hechter, Michael. Internal Colonialism. *The Celtic Fringe in British National Development, 1536-1966. About 350 pp.*
Hertz, Frederick. Nationality in History and Politics: *A Psychology and Sociology of National Sentiment and Nationalism. 432 pp.*

INTERNATIONAL LIBRARY OF SOCIOLOGY

Kornhauser, William. The Politics of Mass Society. *272 pp. 20 tables.*
Laidler, Harry W. History of Socialism. *Social-Economic Movements: An Historical and Comparative Survey of Socialism, Communism, Co-operation, Utopianism; and other Systems of Reform and Reconstruction. 992 pp.*
Lasswell, H. D. Analysis of Political Behaviour. *324 pp.*
Mannheim, Karl. Freedom, Power and Democratic Planning. *Edited by Hans Gerth and Ernest K. Bramstedt. 424 pp.*
Mansur, Fatma. Process of Independence. *Foreword by A. H. Hanson. 208 pp.*
Martin, David A. Pacifism: *an Historical and Sociological Study. 262 pp.*
Myrdal, Gunnar. The Political Element in the Development of Economic Theory. *Translated from the German by Paul Streeten. 282 pp.*
Wootton, Graham. Workers, Unions and the State. *188 pp.*

FOREIGN AFFAIRS: THEIR SOCIAL, POLITICAL AND ECONOMIC FOUNDATIONS

Mayer, J. P. Political Thought in France from the Revolution to the Fifth Republic. *164 pp.*

CRIMINOLOGY

Ancel, Marc. Social Defence: *A Modern Approach to Criminal Problems. Foreword by Leon Radzinowicz. 240 pp.*
Cain, Maureen E. Society and the Policeman's Role. *326 pp.*
Cloward, Richard A., and **Ohlin, Lloyd E.** Delinquency and Opportunity: *A Theory of Delinquent Gangs. 248 pp.*
Downes, David M. The Delinquent Solution. *A Study in Subcultural Theory. 296 pp.*
Dunlop, A. B., and **McCabe, S.** Young Men in Detention Centres. *192 pp.*
Friedlander, Kate. The Psycho-Analytical Approach to Juvenile Delinquency: *Theory, Case Studies, Treatment. 320 pp.*
Glueck, Sheldon, and **Eleanor.** Family Environment and Delinquency. *With the statistical assistance of Rose W. Kneznek. 340 pp.*
Lopez-Rey, Manuel. Crime. *An Analytical Appraisal. 288 pp.*
Mannheim, Hermann. Comparative Criminology: *a Text Book. Two volumes. 442 pp. and 380 pp.*
Morris, Terence. The Criminal Area: *A Study in Social Ecology. Foreword by Hermann Mannheim. 232 pp. 25 tables. 4 maps.*
Rock, Paul. Making People Pay. *338 pp.*
●**Taylor, Ian, Walton, Paul,** and **Young, Jock.** The New Criminology. *For a Social Theory of Deviance. 325 pp.*

SOCIAL PSYCHOLOGY

Bagley, Christopher. The Social Psychology of the Epileptic Child. *320 pp.*
Barbu, Zevedei. Problems of Historical Psychology. *248 pp.*
Blackburn, Julian. Psychology and the Social Pattern. *184 pp.*

INTERNATIONAL LIBRARY OF SOCIOLOGY

● **Brittan, Arthur.** Meanings and Situations. *224 pp.*
Carroll, J. Break-Out from the Crystal Palace. *200 pp.*
● **Fleming, C. M.** Adolescence: Its Social Psychology. *With an Introduction to recent findings from the fields of Anthropology, Physiology, Medicine, Psychometrics and Sociometry. 288 pp.*
● The Social Psychology of Education: *An Introduction and Guide to Its Study. 136 pp.*
Homans, George C. The Human Group. *Foreword by Bernard DeVoto. Introduction by Robert K. Merton. 526 pp.*
● Social Behaviour: *its Elementary Forms. 416 pp.*
● **Klein, Josephine.** The Study of Groups. *226 pp. 31 figures. 5 tables.*
Linton, Ralph. The Cultural Background of Personality. *132 pp.*
● **Mayo, Elton.** The Social Problems of an Industrial Civilization. *With an appendix on the Political Problem. 180 pp.*
Ottaway, A. K. C. Learning Through Group Experience. *176 pp.*
Ridder, J. C. de. The Personality of the Urban African in South Africa. *A Thematic Apperception Test Study. 196 pp. 12 plates.*
● **Rose, Arnold M.** (Ed.) Human Behaviour and Social Processes: *an Interactionist Approach. Contributions by Arnold M. Rose, Ralph H. Turner, Anselm Strauss, Everett C. Hughes, E. Franklin Frazier, Howard S. Becker, et al. 696 pp.*
Smelser, Neil J. Theory of Collective Behaviour. *448 pp.*
Stephenson, Geoffrey M. The Development of Conscience. *128 pp.*
Young, Kimball. Handbook of Social Psychology. *658 pp. 16 figures. 10 tables.*

SOCIOLOGY OF THE FAMILY

Banks, J. A. Prosperity and Parenthood: *A Study of Family Planning among The Victorian Middle Classes. 262 pp.*
Bell, Colin R. Middle Class Families: *Social and Geographical Mobility. 224 pp.*
Burton, Lindy. Vulnerable Children. *272 pp.*
Gavron, Hannah. The Captive Wife: *Conflicts of Household Mothers. 190 pp.*
George, Victor, and **Wilding, Paul.** Motherless Families. *220 pp.*
Klein, Josephine. Samples from English Cultures.
 1. Three Preliminary Studies and Aspects of Adult Life in England. *447 pp.*
 2. Child-Rearing Practices and Index. *247 pp.*
Klein, Viola. Britain's Married Women Workers. *180 pp.*
 The Feminine Character. *History of an Ideology. 244 pp.*
McWhinnie, Alexina M. Adopted Children. *How They Grow Up. 304 pp.*
● **Myrdal, Alva,** and **Klein, Viola.** Women's Two Roles: *Home and Work. 238 pp. 27 tables.*
Parsons, Talcott, and **Bales, Robert F.** Family: Socialization and Interaction Process. *In collaboration with James Olds, Morris Zelditch and Philip E. Slater. 456 pp. 50 figures and tables.*

SOCIAL SERVICES

Bastide, Roger. The Sociology of Mental Disorder. *Translated from the French by Jean McNeil. 260 pp.*
Carlebach, Julius. Caring For Children in Trouble. *266 pp.*
Forder, R. A. (Ed.) Penelope Hall's Social Services of England and Wales. *352 pp.*
George, Victor. Foster Care. *Theory and Practice. 234 pp.*
Social Security: *Beveridge and After. 258 pp.*
George, V., and **Wilding, P.** Motherless Families. *248 pp.*
● **Goetschius, George W.** Working with Community Groups. *256 pp.*
Goetschius, George W., and **Tash, Joan.** Working with Unattached Youth. *416 pp.*
Hall, M. P., and **Howes, I. V.** The Church in Social Work. *A Study of Moral Welfare Work undertaken by the Church of England. 320 pp.*
Heywood, Jean S. Children in Care: *the Development of the Service for the Deprived Child. 264 pp.*
Hoenig, J., and **Hamilton, Marian W.** The De-Segregation of the Mentally Ill. *284 pp.*
Jones, Kathleen. Mental Health and Social Policy, 1845-1959. *264 pp.*
King, Roy D., Raynes, Norma V., and **Tizard, Jack.** Patterns of Residential Care. *356 pp.*
Leigh, John. Young People and Leisure. *256 pp.*
Morris, Mary. Voluntary Work and the Welfare State. *300 pp.*
Morris, Pauline. Put Away: *A Sociological Study of Institutions for the Mentally Retarded. 364 pp.*
Nokes, P. L. The Professional Task in Welfare Practice. *152 pp.*
Timms, Noel. Psychiatric Social Work in Great Britain (1939-1962). *280 pp.*
● Social Casework: *Principles and Practice. 256 pp.*
Young, A. F. Social Services in British Industry. *272 pp.*
Young, A. F., and **Ashton, E. T.** British Social Work in the Nineteenth Century. *288 pp.*

SOCIOLOGY OF EDUCATION

Banks, Olive. Parity and Prestige in English Secondary Education: a Study in Educational Sociology. *272 pp.*
Bentwich, Joseph. Education in Israel. *224 pp. 8 pp. plates.*
● **Blyth, W. A. L.** English Primary Education. *A Sociological Description.*
  1. Schools. *232 pp.*
  2. Background. *168 pp.*
Collier, K. G. The Social Purposes of Education: *Personal and Social Values in Education. 268 pp.*

Dale, R. R., and Griffith, S. Down Stream: *Failure in the Grammar School.* *108 pp.*
Dore, R. P. Education in Tokugawa Japan. *356 pp. 9 pp. plates.*
Evans, K. M. Sociometry and Education. *158 pp.*
●Ford, Julienne. Social Class and the Comprehensive School. *192 pp.*
Foster, P. J. Education and Social Change in Ghana. *336 pp. 3 maps.*
Fraser, W. R. Education and Society in Modern France. *150 pp.*
Grace, Gerald R. Role Conflict and the Teacher. *About 200 pp.*
Hans, Nicholas. New Trends in Education in the Eighteenth Century. *278 pp. 19 tables.*
● Comparative Education: *A Study of Educational Factors and Traditions.* *360 pp.*
Hargreaves, David. Interpersonal Relations and Education. *432 pp.*
● Social Relations in a Secondary School. *240 pp.*
Holmes, Brian. Problems in Education. *A Comparative Approach. 336 pp.*
King, Ronald. Values and Involvement in a Grammar School. *164 pp.*
School Organization and Pupil Involvement. *A Study of Secondary Schools.*
●Mannheim, Karl, and Stewart, W. A. C. An Introduction to the Sociology of Education. *206 pp.*
Morris, Raymond N. The Sixth Form and College Entrance. *231 pp.*
●Musgrove, F. Youth and the Social Order. *176 pp.*
●Ottaway, A. K. C. Education and Society: An Introduction to the Sociology of Education. *With an Introduction by W. O. Lester Smith. 212 pp.*
Peers, Robert. Adult Education: *A Comparative Study. 398 pp.*
Pritchard, D. G. Education and the Handicapped: *1760 to 1960. 258 pp.*
Richardson, Helen. Adolescent Girls in Approved Schools. *308 pp.*
Stratta, Erica. The Education of Borstal Boys. *A Study of their Educational Experiences prior to, and during, Borstal Training. 256 pp.*
Taylor, P. H., Reid, W. A., and Holley, B. J. The English Sixth Form. *A Case Study in Curriculum Research. 200 pp.*

SOCIOLOGY OF CULTURE

Eppel, E. M., and M. Adolescents and Morality: *A Study of some Moral Values and Dilemmas of Working Adolescents in the Context of a changing Climate of Opinion. Foreword by W. J. H. Sprott. 268 pp. 39 tables.*
●Fromm, Erich. The Fear of Freedom. *286 pp.*
● The Sane Society. *400 pp.*
Mannheim, Karl. Essays on the Sociology of Culture. *Edited by Ernst Mannheim in co-operation with Paul Kecskemeti. Editorial Note by Adolph Lowe. 280 pp.*
Weber, Alfred. Farewell to European History: *or The Conquest of Nihilism. Translated from the German by R. F. C. Hull. 224 pp.*

SOCIOLOGY OF RELIGION

Argyle, Michael and **Beit-Hallahmi, Benjamin.** The Social Psychology of Religion. *About 256 pp.*
Nelson, G. K. Spiritualism and Society. *313 pp.*
Stark, Werner. The Sociology of Religion. *A Study of Christendom.*
  Volume I. *Established Religion. 248 pp.*
  Volume II. *Sectarian Religion. 368 pp.*
  Volume III. *The Universal Church. 464 pp.*
  Volume IV. *Types of Religious Man. 352 pp.*
  Volume V. *Types of Religious Culture. 464 pp.*
Turner, B. S. Weber and Islam. *216 pp.*
Watt, W. Montgomery. Islam and the Integration of Society. *320 pp.*

SOCIOLOGY OF ART AND LITERATURE

Jarvie, Ian C. Towards a Sociology of the Cinema. *A Comparative Essay on the Structure and Functioning of a Major Entertainment Industry. 405 pp.*
Rust, Frances S. Dance in Society. *An Analysis of the Relationships between the Social Dance and Society in England from the Middle Ages to the Present Day. 256 pp. 8 pp. of plates.*
Schücking, L. L. The Sociology of Literary Taste. *112 pp.*
Wolff, Janet. Hermeneutic Philosophy and the Sociology of Art. *About 200 pp.*

SOCIOLOGY OF KNOWLEDGE

Diesing, P. Patterns of Discovery in the Social Sciences. *262 pp.*
●**Douglas, J. D.** (Ed.) Understanding Everyday Life. *370 pp.*
●**Hamilton, P.** Knowledge and Social Structure. *174 pp.*
Jarvie, I. C. Concepts and Society. *232 pp.*
Mannheim, Karl. Essays on the Sociology of Knowledge. *Edited by Paul Kecskemeti. Editorial Note by Adolph Lowe. 353 pp.*
Remmling, Gunter W. (Ed.) Towards the Sociology of Knowledge. *Origin and Development of a Sociological Thought Style. 463 pp.*
Stark, Werner. The Sociology of Knowledge: *An Essay in Aid of a Deeper Understanding of the History of Ideas. 384 pp.*

URBAN SOCIOLOGY

Ashworth, William. The Genesis of Modern British Town Planning: *A Study in Economic and Social History of the Nineteenth and Twentieth Centuries. 288 pp.*
Cullingworth, J. B. Housing Needs and Planning Policy: *A Restatement of the Problems of Housing Need and 'Overspill' in England and Wales. 232 pp. 44 tables. 8 maps.*

Dickinson, Robert E. City and Region: *A Geographical Interpretation* 608 pp. *125 figures.*
The West European City: *A Geographical Interpretation.* 600 pp. *129 maps. 29 plates.*
● The City Region in Western Europe. *320 pp. Maps.*
Humphreys, Alexander J. New Dubliners: *Urbanization and the Irish Family. Foreword by George C. Homans.* 304 pp.
Jackson, Brian. Working Class Community: *Some General Notions raised by a Series of Studies in Northern England.* 192 pp.
Jennings, Hilda. Societies in the Making: *a Study of Development and Redevelopment within a County Borough. Foreword by D. A. Clark.* 286 pp.
●**Mann, P. H.** An Approach to Urban Sociology. *240 pp.*
Morris, R. N., and **Mogey, J.** The Sociology of Housing. *Studies at Berinsfield.* 232 pp. *4 pp. plates.*
Rosser, C., and **Harris, C.** The Family and Social Change. *A Study of Family and Kinship in a South Wales Town.* 352 pp. *8 maps.*

RURAL SOCIOLOGY

Chambers, R. J. H. Settlement Schemes in Tropical Africa: *A Selective Study.* 268 pp.
Haswell, M. R. The Economics of Development in Village India. *120 pp.*
Littlejohn, James. Westrigg: *the Sociology of a Cheviot Parish.* 172 pp. *5 figures.*
Mayer, Adrian C. Peasants in the Pacific. *A Study of Fiji Indian Rural Society.* 248 pp. *20 plates.*
Williams, W. M. The Sociology of an English Village: *Gosforth.* 272 pp. *12 figures. 13 tables.*

SOCIOLOGY OF INDUSTRY AND DISTRIBUTION

Anderson, Nels. Work and Leisure. *280 pp.*
●**Blau, Peter M.,** and **Scott, W. Richard.** Formal Organizations: *a Comparative approach. Introduction and Additional Bibliography by J. H. Smith.* 326 pp.
Eldridge, J. E. T. Industrial Disputes. *Essays in the Sociology of Industrial Relations.* 288 pp.
Hetzler, Stanley. Applied Measures for Promoting Technological Growth. *352 pp.*
Technological Growth and Social Change. *Achieving Modernization.* 269 pp.
Hollowell, Peter G. The Lorry Driver. *272 pp.*
Jefferys, Margot, *with the assistance of Winifred Moss.* Mobility in the Labour Market: *Employment Changes in Battersea and Dagenham. Preface by Barbara Wootton.* 186 pp. *51 tables.*

INTERNATIONAL LIBRARY OF SOCIOLOGY

Millerson, Geoffrey. The Qualifying Associations: *a Study in Professionalization. 320 pp.*
Smelser, Neil J. Social Change in the Industrial Revolution: *An Application of Theory to the Lancashire Cotton Industry, 1770-1840. 468 pp. 12 figures. 14 tables.*
Williams, Gertrude. Recruitment to Skilled Trades. *240 pp.*
Young, A. F. Industrial Injuries Insurance: *an Examination of British Policy. 192 pp.*

DOCUMENTARY

Schlesinger, Rudolf (Ed.) Changing Attitudes in Soviet Russia.
2. The Nationalities Problem and Soviet Administration. *Selected Readings on the Development of Soviet Nationalities Policies. Introduced by the editor. Translated by W. W. Gottlieb. 324 pp.*

ANTHROPOLOGY

Ammar, Hamed. Growing up in an Egyptian Village: *Silwa, Province of Aswan. 336 pp.*
Brandel-Syrier, Mia. Reeftown Elite. *A Study of Social Mobility in a Modern African Community on the Reef. 376 pp.*
Crook, David, and **Isabel.** Revolution in a Chinese Village: *Ten Mile Inn. 230 pp. 8 plates. 1 map.*
Dickie-Clark, H. F. The Marginal Situation. *A Sociological Study of a Coloured Group. 236 pp.*
Dube, S. C. Indian Village. *Foreword by Morris Edward Opler. 276 pp. 4 plates.*
 India's Changing Villages: *Human Factors in Community Development. 260 pp. 8 plates. 1 map.*
Firth, Raymond. Malay Fishermen. *Their Peasant Economy. 420 pp. 17 pp. plates.*
Firth, R., Hubert, J., and **Forge, A.** Families and their Relatives. *Kinship in a Middle-Class Sector of London: An Anthropological Study. 456 pp.*
Gulliver, P. H. Social Control in an African Society: a Study of the Arusha, Agricultural Masai of Northern Tanganyika. *320 pp. 8 plates. 10 figures.*
 Family Herds. *288 pp.*
Ishwaran, K. Shivapur. *A South Indian Village. 216 pp.*
 Tradition and Economy in Village India: *An Interactionist Approach. Foreword by Conrad Arensburg. 176 pp.*
Jarvie, Ian C. The Revolution in Anthropology. *268 pp.*
Jarvie, Ian C., and **Agassi, Joseph.** Hong Kong. *A Society in Transition. 396 pp. Illustrated with plates and maps.*
Little, Kenneth L. Mende of Sierra Leone. *308 pp. and folder.*
 Negroes in Britain. *With a New Introduction and Contemporary Study by Leonard Bloom. 320 pp.*

INTERNATIONAL LIBRARY OF SOCIOLOGY

Lowie, Robert H. Social Organization. *494 pp.*
Mayer, Adrian, C. Caste and Kinship in Central India: *A Village and its Region. 328 pp. 16 plates. 15 figures. 16 tables.*
Peasants in the Pacific. *A Study of Fiji Indian Rural Society. 248 pp.*
Smith, Raymond T. The Negro Family in British Guiana: *Family Structure and Social Status in the Villages. With a Foreword by Meyer Fortes. 314 pp. 8 plates. 1 figure. 4 maps.*

SOCIOLOGY AND PHILOSOPHY

Barnsley, John H. The Social Reality of Ethics. *A Comparative Analysis of Moral Codes. 448 pp.*
Diesing, Paul. Patterns of Discovery in the Social Sciences. *362 pp.*
●**Douglas, Jack D.** (Ed.) Understanding Everyday Life. *Toward the Reconstruction of Sociological Knowledge. Contributions by Alan F. Blum. Aaron W. Cicourel, Norman K. Denzin, Jack D. Douglas, John Heeren, Peter McHugh, Peter K. Manning, Melvin Power, Matthew Speier, Roy Turner, D. Lawrence Wieder, Thomas P. Wilson and Don H. Zimmerman. 370 pp.*
Jarvie, Ian C. Concepts and Society. *216 pp.*
Pelz, Werner. The Scope of Understanding in Sociology. *Towards a more radical reorientation in the social humanistic sciences. 283 pp.*
Roche, Maurice. Phenomenology, Language and the Social Sciences. *371 pp.*
Sahay, Arun. Sociological Analysis. *212 pp.*
Sklair, Leslie. The Sociology of Progress. *320 pp.*

International Library of Anthropology
General Editor Adam Kuper

Brown, Paula. The Chimbu. *A Study of Change in the New Guinea Highlands. 151 pp.*
Lloyd, P. C. Power and Independence. *Urban Africans' Perception of Social Inequality. 264 pp.*
Pettigrew, Joyce. Robber Noblemen. *A Study of the Political System of the Sikh Jats. 284 pp.*
Van Den Berghe, Pierre L. Power and Privilege at an African University. *278 pp.*

International Library of Social Policy
General Editor Kathleen Jones

Bayley, M. Mental Handicap and Community Care. *426 pp.*
Butler, J. R. Family Doctors and Public Policy. *208 pp.*
Holman, Robert. Trading in Children. *A Study of Private Fostering. 355 pp.*

INTERNATIONAL LIBRARY OF SOCIAL POLICY

Jones, Kathleen. History of the Mental Health Service. *428 pp.*
Thomas, J. E. The English Prison Officer since 1850: *A Study in Conflict. 258 pp.*
Woodward, J. To Do the Sick No Harm. *A Study of the British Voluntary Hospital System to 1875. About 220 pp.*

International Library of Welfare and Philosophy
General Editors Noel Timms and David Watson

● **Plant, Raymond.** Community and Ideology. *104 pp.*

Primary Socialization, Language and Education
General Editor Basil Bernstein

Bernstein, Basil. Class, Codes and Control. *2 volumes.*
  1. *Theoretical Studies Towards a Sociology of Language. 254 pp.*
  2. *Applied Studies Towards a Sociology of Language. About 400 pp.*
Brandis, W., and **Bernstein, B.** Selection and Control. *176 pp.*
Brandis, Walter, and **Henderson, Dorothy.** Social Class, Language and Communication. *288 pp.*
Cook-Gumperz, Jenny. Social Control and Socialization. *A Study of Class Differences in the Language of Maternal Control. 290 pp.*
● **Gahagan, D. M.,** and **G. A.** Talk Reform. *Exploration in Language for Infant School Children. 160 pp.*
Robinson, W. P., and **Rackstraw, Susan D. A.** A Question of Answers. *2 volumes. 192 pp. and 180 pp.*
Turner, Geoffrey J., and **Mohan, Bernard A.** A Linguistic Description and Computer Programme for Children's Speech. *208 pp.*

Reports of the Institute of Community Studies

Cartwright, Ann. Human Relations and Hospital Care. *272 pp.*
● Parents and Family Planning Services. *306 pp.*
  Patients and their Doctors. *A Study of General Practice. 304 pp.*
● **Jackson, Brian.** Streaming: *an Education System in Miniature. 168 pp.*
Jackson, Brian, and **Marsden, Dennis.** Education and the Working Class: *Some General Themes raised by a Study of 88 Working-class Children in a Northern Industrial City. 268 pp. 2 folders.*
Marris, Peter. The Experience of Higher Education. *232 pp. 27 tables.*
  Loss and Change. *192 pp.*

Marris, Peter, and Rein, Martin. Dilemmas of Social Reform. *Poverty and Community Action in the United States*. 256 pp.
Marris, Peter, and Somerset, Anthony. African Businessmen. *A Study of Entrepreneurship and Development in Kenya*. 256 pp.
Mills, Richard. Young Outsiders: *a Study in Alternative Communities*. 216 pp.
Runciman, W. G. Relative Deprivation and Social Justice. *A Study of Attitudes to Social Inequality in Twentieth-Century England*. 352 pp.
Willmott, Peter. Adolescent Boys in East London. *230 pp.*
Willmott, Peter, and Young, Michael. Family and Class in a London Suburb. *202 pp. 47 tables.*
Young, Michael. Innovation and Research in Education. *192 pp.*
●Young, Michael, and McGeeney, Patrick. Learning Begins at Home. *A Study of a Junior School and its Parents*. 128 pp.
Young, Michael, and Willmott, Peter. Family and Kinship in East London. Foreword by Richard M. Titmuss. *252 pp. 39 tables.*
The Symmetrical Family. *410 pp.*

Reports of the Institute for Social Studies in Medical Care

Cartwright, Ann, Hockey, Lisbeth, and Anderson, John L. Life Before Death. *310 pp.*
Dunnell, Karen, and Cartwright, Ann. Medicine Takers, Prescribers and Hoarders. *190 pp.*

Medicine, Illness and Society
General Editor W. M. Williams

Robinson, David. The Process of Becoming Ill. *142 pp.*
Stacey, Margaret, *et al*. Hospitals, Children and Their Families. *The Report of a Pilot Study*. 202 pp.

Monographs in Social Theory
General Editor Arthur Brittan

●Barnes, B. Scientific Knowledge and Sociological Theory. *About 200 pp.*
Bauman, Zygmunt. Culture as Praxis. *204 pp.*
●Dixon, Keith. Sociological Theory. *Pretence and Possibility*. 142 pp.
●Smith, Anthony D. The Concept of Social Change. *A Critique of the Functionalist Theory of Social Change*. 208 pp.

Routledge Social Science Journals

The British Journal of Sociology. *Edited by Terence P. Morris. Vol. 1, No. 1, March 1950 and Quarterly. Roy. 8vo. Back numbers available. An international journal with articles on all aspects of sociology.*

Economy and Society. *Vol. 1, No. 1. February 1972 and Quarterly. Metric Roy. 8vo. A journal for all social scientists covering sociology, philosophy, anthropology, economics and history. Back numbers available.*

Year Book of Social Policy in Britain, The. *Edited by Kathleen Jones. 1971. Published annually.*

Printed in Great Britain by Unwin Brothers Limited
The Gresham Press Old Woking Surrey
A member of the Staples Printing Group